Praise for
Brian D. Mahan, SEP
and *I Cried All the
Way to Happy Hour*

"Simply a must-read. Brian's compassion, wisdom and humor leap off the page, guiding us onto a path of profound healing and transformation."

- Marie Forleo
#1 New York Times bestseller
Everything is Figureoutable

"Brian is a profoundly talented practitioner and deeply committed to helping people heal from trauma. I'm proud to call him a teacher and a friend."

- Gabby Bernstein
#1 New York Times bestselling author of
The Universe has Your Back

"In one session Brian took the physical manifestation of my trauma and healed it. That ball of pain that lived in my body for so long literally left and never came back! His work and his teachings are game changing."

- Maria Menounos
2x New York Times best selling author and host of
Better Together with Maria Menounos

"Brian Mahan writes like a force of nature, like he has something truly important to tell us, which thankfully he does! Not only through training, but through experience—both laugh-out-loud funny and terrifying—Brian weaves personal experience with his deep knowledge of Somatic Experiencing to bring you a road map for healing your most profound traumas. Thank you, Brian, for this remarkable gift."

- Matthew Carnahan
creator of Emmy Award-winning series *HOUSE OF LIES* and
author of *SERPENT GIRL*

"Brian creates a safe space to start with the "facts" of your traumas. Then with brilliant compassion he helps you develop an acute awareness of the physiology of what's happening in your body. At first glance, it seems like you're just helplessly looking at the pain. And then you realize—it's an unfailing tool that masterfully releases it."

- Nicole Ari Parker
Actor, Producer, Parent

"Brian has the profound ability to lead me towards the truth. Always."

- Annabelle Dexter Jones
(HBO *'Succession'*) Actor, Director

"Traditional therapy made me relive my trauma by having to tell the same story again and again, without seeing any improvement. Brian takes you to the core issues in a whole new way so that you actually heal!"

- Tamar Geller
New York Times best selling author of *The Loved Dog and as Oprah says*, "A Life Coach for Dogs and their People"

I CRIED ALL THE WAY TO HAPPY HOUR

Foreword by Jonathan Salk, M.D.

To request permission, contact the author at
BrianDMahanSEP@gmail.com

Hardcover: ISBN 978-0-578-39487-9
Paperback: ISBN 978-0-578-39486-2
Audiobook: coming soon
Updates and more info:
www.BrianDMahanBook.com

Library of Congress Number: TBD

First paperback edition March 2020.

Edited by Wandering Words
Cover art and Layout by Aaniyah Ahmed

www.BrianDMahan.com
www.BrianDMahanBook.com
All social media @BrianDMahanSEP

Dedication

To my mother, I can't express the gratitude I feel knowing that we have repaired our relationship and that you are now proud of me.

To my father, a great lover of books who is not here to read this one: it pains me that you never knew whom I came to be nor how I now live my life.

To my Boobi-baby-boobala, Barbara Quinton, you have always been my soft spot to land, supporter-in-chief, and my bestest best friend. There really are no words.

BNX - 11:11! Where would we be without each other?

To Joel, who remained patient and supportive withstanding the neglect that came with my determination to finish writing this book. I love you.

A Personal Note to You

I would bet my bottom dollar that you have already tried many ways to change and heal. You probably feel as though you have made progress, but you just can't seem to cross the finish line. And now, you are searching for the missing link. You may be questioning yourself for even picking this book up, afraid that it, too, won't get you to where you want to be. I'm sure that you're exasperated and might even feel like you are broken beyond repair.

You're not.

I see you, I hear you, I get you, I acknowledge you, and I appreciate you. I empathize and sympathize with you. I feel great compassion for you.

I don't want to make any false or exaggerated promises, and I want you to have realistic expectations. Healing does take time. I won't tell you that reading this book is all that you will need to do, but I can guarantee that, by doing so, you will save yourself an enormous amount of time and money and fast-track your personal transformation.

The good news is that all of your prior introspection, self-help exploration, and therapeutic approaches have had enormous benefits in creating the scaffolding needed for your transformation.

Up until this point, you survived. You learned, and you grew. You entangled and untangled. You stumbled and got back on your feet again. You got stuck, you quit, and you found the resolve to engage again. You bent, cracked, and nearly broke, and, as best as you could, you soldered yourself back together and soldiered on. Now, you strive to thrive again.

Like a blacksmith through his own sweat and tears, the people and experiences of your life have forged the fingerprint that you have come to be. All the potential of who you could have been was melted down and slowly poured into a mold that was much too small. At times, the whirl of the world guided you gently—at other times, it rammed into you with nearly unimaginable force. The furnace of others' expectations pitted themselves against your natural tendencies and genetically encoded predeterminations. The metal of your character has been hammered into place, regardless of if by care and nurturing or by the intentional demand for you to change shape.

In response, you became entrenched within a unique kaleidoscope of defenses, coping mechanisms, survival strategies, unconscious embodied beliefs, and subsequent repetitive behaviors.

I got into the work, first, as a client. I went from living a life of dissociation, angst, unbreakable patterns, and full-blown panic attacks to one of self-confidence, self-esteem, empowerment, embodiment, and joyfulness.

But for decades, I had been an insatiable seeker. By hook or by crook, I was determined to stop being my Self. I tried everything I could think of to try to feel better. And, truthfully, I didn't even know what was wrong with me—but something was seriously wrong with me.

I read every self-help book I could get my hands on—except for that one on self-sabotage. I never finished it. I sought the guidance of a plethora of therapists, self-help visionaries, healers, psychics, kahunas, and even a witch doctor (yes, really). I became a human guinea pig and gobbled down every pill, potion, and powder known to man. I filled journal after journal after journal. I attended dozens and dozens of workshops and retreats. I sat at the foot of many a guru (G-U-R-U) and fervently prayed. I took countless hours of yoga and meditated and medicated myself into a stupor. Yet, try as I might to heal my inner child and embrace my feminine side and do everything else they told me I should do, time and time again, my 'isms' kept kicking my dogmas to the curb.

So, needless to say, I have been there, done that. Got the T-shirt, the merit badge, and the bumper sticker.

But, here's the thing: even if you had all the dentistry textbooks and tools, I don't think you should attempt to fill your own cavities. And I'm sure your dental hygienist isn't who you would choose to perform a root canal. What I mean by this is, in time, you may find that you need to avail yourself of the right kind of professional support.

I understand that most trauma survivors want the process of healing to be over and done with, like yesterday. Let me be frank with you. There is no magic carpet ride. There is no one-size-fits-all formula. There isn't a step-by-step process or simple equation you can follow and then rinse and repeat. However, there are some fundamental basics and universal truths that, when deftly leveraged, can unlock and release you quickly from the bondage of that which you were informed by and have been formed into.

If you are currently in crisis, the resources available online are filled with straightforward tools, skills, and resources for quick and easy reference. Perhaps you may want to start experimenting with a few of them in order to find some immediate relief. Also, don't be surprised if reading some of my narrative or the other case studies is activating or triggering for you. If you find that to be the case, take a break and practice The 5's Open-Eyed Moving Meditation™ to orient yourself to the present moment.[1]

---

[1] Mahan, B. D. (2022, March 8). Resources and tools for I Cried All the Way To Happy Hour. Access Resources for I Cried All the Way to Happy Hour. Retrieved March 8, 2022, from https://briandmahansep2022.ck.page/ad51dbb5db

Contents

PART TWO

MYTH BUSTING
What Won't Help and Why

PART THREE

BUILDING THE FOUNDATION
FOR HEALING

Foreword

Trauma and toxic shame. These two potent contributors to human suffering, dysfunction and pain have, in recent decades, come to the forefront of our thinking about mental health and personal healing. For many scientists and practitioners this has resulted in advances in the understanding and treatment of emotional pain and distress.

The role of the body in our experience and in the processing of deep emotions has also come into focus in the same period and, as a result, has become the basis of a number of therapies and healing activities. This unity of mind and body has always been central to both mental and physical health, but the understanding that all experience, especially traumatic experience, is recorded and stored in the nerves and muscles and connective tissue of the body is a truly revolutionary awareness that has led to ever more effective techniques for healing and growth.

Recently, we have expanded the meaning of trauma to include not only situations beyond the realm of ordinary human experience that threaten life or physical safety but also common situations in early development such as emotionally toxic environments, verbal assault and shame. The body does not only record the larger traumas; the smaller insults, slights, judgements, humiliations are all stored in the brain and body as well – impeding true health and, as we find in this book, joy.

These themes are interwoven in Brian Mahan's account of his personal journey and his sharing of the knowledge and wisdom he has acquired over a lifetime of searching, learning and healing. Drawing heavily on Peter Levine's seminal work in Somatic Experiencing and Brett Lyon, Sheila Rubin and Brene Brown's work in toxic shame, he weaves his own tapestry of development, psychology, physiology, neurobiology and human relationship.

Notably, he does not present himself as a guru or master with a one-size-fits-all recipe for growth and success. He does not try to create and sell a product or brand. Instead, he tells the story in a non-didactic, narrative way, as if the reader were in his consultation room (or on Zoom), face to face, as he explains the concepts on which his work is based and with which he, with notable success, heals psychic and somatic injury. He then recommends that each reader find a teacher or therapist who is compassionate and skilled at the accessing, resolving and healing of toxic shame and trauma at the deepest levels of mind and body.

He tells us at the outset that his goal is to guide the reader toward a path of healing and integration. You will be the final judge, but I believe he has succeeded.

Jonathan D. Salk, M.D.
Psychiatrist in private practice and Assistant Clinical Professor of Psychiatry at the UCLA David Geffen School of Medicine

Acknowledgments

In deep gratitude for all who wounded me, including the driver of the car that hit me and kept going or those who have triggered the wounded parts of me. You provided me with my learning, growth, and healing edges. Without you, I would not be the man I am today.

My eternal thanks to all of my past, present, and future clients. You have taught me so much about the meaning of life, the resilience of human beings, and inspired me to continue to heal and help others heal.

I cannot express the breadth and depth of my love and appreciation for my fRamily (my family of friends)—the gaggle of co-conspirators and comrades who love and accept me, regardless of my shortcomings. You have shown me what unconditional love truly is. Although we are not related by blood, we are through laughter, deep conversation, and the safety we feel from knowing that we have each others' backs.

I would not be able to help others had it not been for my teachers and healers, of which there are too many to name. There is a special place in my heart for the faculty, administrators, and assistant trainers at the Somatic Experiencing International, including but not limited to Dr. Peter A. Levine, Raja Selvam, Maggie Kline, Abi Blakeslee, Beverly Buehner, and Dr. Connie O'Reilly. I respect and revere Bret Lyon, Sheila Rubin, and The Center for Healing Shame. You all have changed me.

There are two things that I will never understand—how anyone has ever had a second child or written a second book. I am humbled and blessed by those who have contributed, endorsed, and supported me during the process of writing this book, including but not limited to: the editors at Wandering Words Media: Qat Wanders, Allison Goddard, and Christina Bagni, my book promoter Tony Scott of Ngage people, and my patient and tireless cover and interior designer, Aaniyah Ahmed. And, special thanks from the bottom of my heart for the generous support from the amazingly talented Maria Menounos, Marie Forleo, Gabby Bernstein, Matthew Carnahan, Nicole Ari Parker, Annabelle Dexter-Jones, Tamar Geller, and Jonathan Salk, M.D.

And thank you to everyone who along the way simply asked, "How's the book coming along?"

The Story of the Title

I asked my client, a woman who worked in politics, "What, if anything, do you remember about our first session—and how, if at all, has it played out over time?"

She leaned forward in her chair, squinted her eyes, and took a slow, intentional breath. She looked deep into my eyes as if I were a lobbyist whose agenda threatened her constituents. The corners of her mouth curled as her brow furrowed, revealing a career of staring down adversaries. I swallowed hard, wondering if I had, perhaps, misspoken during our first meeting.

The long dramatic pause ended with, "I'm not a crier. I don't cry." She paused again. "But last time, when I left here . . . I had to meet a colleague for cocktails." Tossing her head to one side, she added, "And I cried all the way to happy hour."

Snorting may not have been the best response, but snorting is rarely something one puts a lot of thought into.

My uncontrollable laughter clearly caught her off guard. As if she received a physical blow to her body, she collapsed into the suede wingback chair. Her eyes opened wide, and her mouth remained agape after a fast and full inhalation.

When I could catch my breath, I asked politely, "May I repeat that back to you?"

Hesitantly, I mirrored verbatim what she had said to me: "I'm not a crier. I don't cry. But last time when I left here, I had to meet a colleague for cocktails, and I cried all the way to happy hour."

She let out a howl of laughter that overshadowed my own. Her stony veneer was no match for genuine human interconnection. In an instant, we were laughing together like old friends reliving an inside joke. The more I laughed, the more she laughed. I could see on her face that she hadn't shared a moment like that with anyone in a very long time.

As we both wiped tears of joy from our eyes, I asked, "May I have that? I think that is the title of my book."

PART ONE

INTRODUCTION

My Story

The Best Thing That Ever Happened to Me

*I*t was December 21, 2003, at around 7:00 p.m. The I-10S freeway was packed with last-minute shoppers. Aspen, my sidekick cocker spaniel, had come along for what she thought would be a joy ride. Dog was my co-pilot.

I was keeping up with the flow of traffic, staying between the dividing white lines of the second lane, and had plenty of room between me and the car ahead of me.

Suddenly, something shot by me at such high velocity I couldn't even imagine what it could be. Reflexively, my eyes darted to the rearview mirror to orient to my environment in a futile attempt to figure out what the hell was going on. Then, I heard an insanely loud sound behind me—the engine of a high-performance sports car downshifting as it tried to swerve around me. It was the second of two racing, like out of the movie, The Fast and the Furious. One of the witnesses said that she thought that the car that hit me was red, but it was going too fast to tell for sure.

My eyes never completed their trajectory to the rearview mirror. Instead, they became transfixed on Aspen, who was standing on the car's instrument panel! I could practically smell the smoke from the gears of my mind grinding to a halt. My conscious mind grappled with how she could be standing on a vertical surface.

But my lower reptilian brain took command over the situation, even before my higher brain could figure out that I was in trouble. Within a millisecond, my body was flushed with warmth as my system flooded with endorphins, dopamine, adrenaline, serotonin, and whatever else my body's pharmacology had at its disposal. All my five senses became heightened. Time seemed to slow down, so much so that I was left hanging in suspended animation. I felt the air in the car get thick as molasses. My eyesight became crystal clear, capturing the finest details. My field of vision expanded as if I were looking through a fisheye lens. The sounds of metal meeting concrete and glass shattering enveloped me like a Dolby surround sound theater.

Then, I felt as though two great big arms wrapped themselves around me, and I heard a man's voice outside of my head speaking into my left ear. I had grown accustomed to hearing voices inside my head, but this was entirely different.

On the back of my neck, I felt hot air as the voice, quite matter-of-factly, told me, "There is nothing you can do anymore. Just let go."

My head whipped around to see who was in the back seat whispering in my ear. There was no one there. What else was I to do but heed the advice of the phantom voice? Without hesitation, I took my hands off of the steering wheel and my foot off of the brake.

Aspen was frozen, still standing on the speedometer. The car was nose down at that point. That which was once a vertical surface had become a horizontal one.

I peered deeply into my sweet Aspen's hollow stare and said, "Everything is going to be okay. Come here," while patting my legs gently.

She, too, was stuck in time. But she slowly crawled down into the wheel well and made her way underneath my knees, shaking like a leaf. I patted her head and her rump to reassure her . . . and myself. I then covered my head with my arms, holding the back of my head with my hands. Had I been limber enough, I would have put my head between my knees and kissed my ass goodbye.

I had a moment of unshakeable clarity: I was going to die.

For years, I had often compared my life to Mr. Toad's Wild Ride, and now the children's tale was coming true. My catchphrase had been 'Stop the world. I want to get off.' My opportunity had come.

I remember taking a great big deep breath. On the most satisfying sigh of my life, I was surprised to hear, "Finally," escaping from my mouth.

I saw the image of a little red schoolhouse in my mind's eye, which I interpreted as a symbol that my life's lessons were coming to an end.

I'm graduating from Earth's School of Hard Knocks, I thought to myself.

And never before, or since, have I been so 'in the moment' and 'present.' I was so relieved . . . calm . . . at peace. I was, instantaneously, fully surrendered to the notion that I was going to die. And I was relieved! In fact, I felt a bit excited. I had no fear whatsoever, as my car flipped in slow motion, end over end, rolling sideways three times across three lanes of traffic and sliding on the driver's door 150 feet before crashing into a concrete wall.

I didn't see my life pass before my eyes. Instead, my first thought was, *Why did I ever quit smoking?* I had quit a few years prior in fear that it would eventually kill me. And this was how

I was going to die?! I felt ripped off. And I was pissed.

I listened to the sound of crunching metal and waited for the impact that would surely kill us.

The next thought was, *Oh, I'm so glad I got all of my Christmas gift bags done.*

And then, *Oh no! I'm going to be one of those tragic Christmas stories!*

Now, every year my friends would get together and remember how I had died right before Christmas.

No, they won't, I thought next, immediately contradicting myself with the hard-nosed reality.

Maybe a few would at first, but my friends' and family's lives would go on, and I would soon perish from their awareness, only to reappear on occasion in a wistful moment.

But what about my house and all my stuff?

And then, none of it mattered anymore. Nothing. Nada. Zilch. It could all go in the landfill. My bills and belongings didn't matter. I didn't care about the mess I was leaving behind. It would all get sorted out one way or another. The details and circumstances of my little life were rendered irrelevant.

Upside down; right side up; upside down; right side up; upside down.

A cascade of thoughts flickered through my mind, *This is surely going to be a multiple car pile-up. God, I hope no one else is injured. I wonder how many cars will be involved. Why is my shoulder so hot? That's weird. Why is my shoulder so hot?*

Broken glass danced slowly around me.

After careful consideration, I hypothesized that it must be due to it dragging on the pavement.

To test my presumption, I rolled my shoulder slightly forward and the searing white-hot pain abated. Yup! That's it!

The squeal of screeching tires sounded far away; the stench of burned rubber permeated me.

BOOM!

The concrete retaining wall had proven the theory of inertia. Had it not been there, I would have gone over the embankment and landed on the roof of an apartment building.

But, alas, I had come to rest, hanging upside down. The car filled with smoke. And, patiently, I continued to wait for my release. I was so intrigued and excited to discover what the death experience was going to be like.

Then the voice came back, but this time spoke with a tone of urgency, "You need to turn the engine off. Now!"

For the first time, I felt fear. Time sped back up to normal. Panic coursed through my veins. Disoriented by my upside-down world, I scrambled to find the key. But when I found it, I couldn't get it to turn.

Suddenly, I realized that I had a choice. Turn the key and live, or don't and be set free.

But my survival instinct had taken over. My body was already in motion. I felt the key begin to bend under the adrenaline-filled torque that I was applying. I could have easily broken it off in the ignition.

Then the damn voice came back one final time, condescending yet grave and determined: "It's in Drive," he said firmly as if to imply, "You fucking idiot!"

It seemed even my guardian angel, or whatever it was, had a propensity toward sarcasm, too.

Fear won out, and I had already learned to listen to the voice. Reluctantly, I shifted the gear into Park and turned the key.

Then, I heard other voices and footsteps as a group of people scurried toward the wreckage. I watched feet kicking at the windshield, which was a bit excessive, as all of the other windows had been blown out. I passed my trembling, sweet girl out of the back passenger's window into the welcoming arms of an anonymous man, who I will never be able to thank appropriately. So kind was he to deliver her to my partner's home.

(Historically, whenever I have shared the story of that one fateful winter night, everyone always asks about Aspen. Everyone is apparently most concerned with her experience of the event. So, for your peace of mind: although she wasn't injured, sadly, she was never the same. She went deaf that night, never quit trembling, and refused to ever roll over again for belly rubs.)

Like a phoenix rising out of Humpty Dumpty's broken shell, I followed Aspen's suit and climbed out of the escape hatch, reluctantly, back into reality. I waited for the police, ambulance, and tow truck to arrive, barefoot and laughing and cutting jokes with those who remained with me.

No other cars were involved. The car that hit me kept going, and the driver was never caught.

It was just for me.

I walked away with just a little road rash on my left shoulder and elbow and a bit of whiplash. And I was so pissed off that I was still alive.

But that was just the beginning of the best thing that has ever happened to me.

Walking the Razor's Edge

*M*y astrological chart has always surprised astrologers when they looked it over. It has been explained to me that nearly all of my planets are in three houses, which is called a Triple Grand Trine. One astrologer told me that it is a very rare aspect that I actually share with Gandhi, Jesus, and Hitler. It's always made me feel like a gross underachiever. And it is probably best not to piss me off.

It did make me think, though—if the wreck were just for me, and I had survived, then what did that mean? Could it be that my survival was a sign that my Triple Grand Trine life had purpose, after all? If so, I had better get busy.

I don't remember much about the ensuing days and weeks following the car wreck. It's still very much a blur. I can't recall how long it was between the time of the wreck and the time that I sought help. I honestly don't have a reference point. All I remember is that, initially, I lay holed up in my apartment in the middle of the living room floor, curled up into the fetal position, howling at the moon with the drapes drawn, the lights off, my phone turned on silent, and the door locked.

I wondered if I was cracking up. I was too afraid to call anyone and tell them what I was going through because I did not want to be committed, as I had already escaped that sentence the night of my nearly nervous breakdown in 1991. I had canceled all of my appointments, concerned that if my clients knew what had happened, they would assume I was not fit to work. In truth, I wasn't. I was a healer, and since I couldn't heal myself, I didn't feel like I had anything to offer.

I felt ashamed that I had wanted to die, yet venom welled up inside of me at the prospect of having to go on living. Not only did I face the monotony of the normal challenges of day-to-day existence, but also, I now had the added burden of finding a new car, filing insurance claims, and holding my proverbial shit together.

Then, to add insult to injury, during my maiden voyage back out into the world, I had the first of dozens of panic attacks.

Or maybe it was just one long panic attack that lasted for several days. I didn't even know at the time what they were—but regardless, I found myself spending much of my commute, as I tried to make my way to the doctor and physical therapy three days a week in my Rent-A-Wreck, on the shoulder of the road, pummeling the steering wheel or my thighs with both fists in an effort to collect myself, not knowing how I was going to get off the freeway and back to the sanctuary of my darkened apartment. It took an inordinate amount of time to discover that the trigger for these events was simply a car passing me, which can be quite problematic considering that 'nobody walks in LA.'

I didn't know what was happening to me. My emotions ran amuck, vacillating between terror, anger, and despondency. I felt like I was going to come undone at the seams as if I would burst into a billion tiny pieces.

There was no advanced warning, but, seven to ten times a day, I would find myself shaking so hard I could hear my bones rattle—and, try as I might, I couldn't stop it. I sat on my hands, laid on my arms, squeezed my legs together, curled into the tightest ball that I could. My heart would race a hundred miles an hour as if it would crack through my ribs and end up on my lap. I couldn't catch my breath—my lungs were on fire, and a large purple vein running down the center of my forehead felt as though it were about to detonate.

I muffled my screams to avoid having the neighbors call the police and bawled my eyes out like a jilted schoolgirl. I experienced tunnel vision that distorted things like the peephole in my Manhattan apartment, which could make Mother Teresa look like a gangbanger.

I had heard recovering alcoholics tell the stories of how, during their 'slips,' they didn't pick up drinking where they had 'left off.' Rather, it was as if the disease had continued and even grown during their abstinence. Similarly, everything I thought I had healed over the past 25 years had come back in spades. I feared that all the good parts of me got to leave and all the bad parts of me remained behind. It was as if the impact of the car wreck had shaken loose everything I had compartmentalized for so many years. Everything I had suppressed, everything I had packed into tidy boxes, tied up with a bow, and stored on a high shelf in the recesses of my mind, came crashing down around me. I lay writhing on the floor among the carnage of all I had been.

I thought my head would explode from the deafening screaming of internal voices. I was utterly hopeless and so angry that I had survived the wreck, and not only was I still here, but now I had to, once again, deal with everything I had tried so diligently to heal from for so many years. All of my negative cyclical thinking, old core beliefs, self-doubt, self-loathing, character defects, shortcomings, self-destructive patterns, and habits had returned in full force. It seemed as though all I had managed to do was gain some cognitive perspective and a little time, distance, and space from all my symptoms and struggles. With all of them back, what was I to do now?

In my delusional mania, I had convinced myself that when I had accepted that I was going to die during the car wreck, I must have entered into the place between here and the hereafter. Something evil or demonic must have attached to me. I came to what seemed to be the most logical conclusion: I had become possessed. This had been a deep-seated fear of mine since my parents took me to see The Exorcist when I was eight years old—truly one of the more traumatic events of my formative years. I still can't understand how I was even allowed to enter the theater.

And now, my worst fear seemed to be coming true. I wanted to nip this in the bud before my head spun around and I began to spit pea soup.

If there was anyone who could help me, I knew who it was. So I peeled myself off of the floor, forced my way across town, and crumpled into the arms of Dr. Connie, who had been my go-to health provider for years. She had seen me through so much but had certainly never seen me like this. I summoned up the courage and asked if she could refer me to an exorcist.

By the grace of God, she laughed and said, "Honey . . . what's going on?"

After several minutes of patient and active listening, she chortled and said, "Baaaby, you don't need an exorcist; you need a trauma specialist."

"A trauma specialist? Sounds expensive."

She gave me the name of a Somatic Experiencing practitioner. I remembered that a friend had just told me that the 'pain and suffering' part of my insurance claim could be as much as three times the cost of my medical expenses. I made the call with dollar signs in my eyes.

Thank God I hadn't gone to see a priest.

Comedy
and
Trauma

The car wreck is by far the single most significant incident in my life. It has become a mile marker of the great divide between who I once was and the man I am today. I think of my life prior to the accident as 'B.C.' and afterward as 'A.D.'

It was as if the divine guidance of a lifetime of trials and tribulations had led me to that particular intersection of longitude and latitude on the face of planet Earth at that precise nanosecond in time. And within that moment of providence, the conflation of my fate and all that I had ever known recalibrated and confirmed my destiny.

But, before we go any further, perhaps you will find it insightful to discover a bit more about how the seemingly random people and experiences of my early life were, in fact, all a part of a perfectly woven tapestry of kismet.

I grew up in the Bible Belt, but we did not go to church, except from time to time for a holiday service. The only proof of that is a black-and-white photo of my two older brothers and me dressed up in our Easter suits with short pants, huddled around our glamorous mother, frocked in her Sunday best with her hair teased and Aqua Netted into submission. And I have one fuzzy memory of Sunday School that hangs on in a ghostly manner.

Fade in:

A plump face of a saccharine-sweet woman sporting the-higher-the-hair-the-closer-to-God bouffant hairdo, struggling to hold its shape until her next wash and set at the beauty parlor. She led us in song, her singing voice as sharp as the corners of her cat-eye glasses.

Jesus Loves the Little Children

Words by C. Herbert Woolston, music by George F. Root

Jesus loves the little children

All the children of the world

Red, brown, yellow

Black and white

They are precious in His sight.

Jesus loves the little children

Of the world.

Jesus died for all the children

All the children of the world

Red, brown, yellow

Black and white

They are precious in His sight.

Jesus died for all the children

Of the world.

Jesus rose for all the children

All the children of the world

Red, brown, yellow

Black and white

They are precious in His sight.

Jesus rose for all the children

Of the world.

I was barely whispering the lyrics, confused by who this Jesus fellow was and why he would love me of all people. I didn't even remember ever meeting him.

And what really perplexed me most was why he had died for me. What did I do that was so wrong? And when I looked around the room, there weren't any red, brown, yellow, or black children. Were they on the outside looking in? No, I didn't see any red, brown, yellow, or black noses pressed against the window panes.

Fade out.

Above the chalkboard in one of my elementary school teacher's classrooms hung a painting of a small boy kneeling in prayer. At the bottom in ornate, almost-illegible-to-me calligraphy were the words, 'If you really want your prayers to be answered, get off your knees.' So perplexed by the juxtaposition of the image and the message, I was repeatedly admonished for daydreaming and moved to the front row, bringing me even closer to my quandary.

One place I felt safe was in the embrace of our housekeeper, Miss Bula, who had the most beautiful skin, as black as cast iron and as soft as spun cotton. She attended church services three times a week. I would often see her with the other 'colored folk,' with their dog-eared Bibles that looked older than they were tucked under their arms or open wide while they waited for the bus. They fervently reread passages over and over, convinced that the good word would be made manifest in their lives. I couldn't make sense of how their prayers never seemed to be answered. After all, the white people only went to church for an hour a week, when they would take their Bibles out of the trunks of their cars, yet all of their lives seemed to be rich with His glory. And my father's mentor and best friend was Jewish, but his faith kept him from being able to have lunch with my father at the Norfolk Yacht & Country Club. Religion remained a mystery to me as I slowly collected shards of overheard adult conversations. It was like trying to put together a jigsaw puzzle that was not intended for my age group and was also missing pieces that had been lost under the sofa cushions or placed in the wrong box.

I had always been pensive and withdrawn. I simply couldn't make sense of the world around me. There were many rules and just as many contradictions, and I just never felt like I fit in or belonged anywhere, not even within my own family.

At about seven years old, I had my first bout of talk therapy. I recall session after session, lying on a brocade couch in a dimly lit room, listening to the sound of a ballpoint pen scratching incessantly across paper punctuated by the sounds of the turning pages. My therapist sat in a chair behind me, off to the right, and just barely out of sight. For that, I was grateful. The moments that I would crane my neck to look back to make sure that he was keeping a safe distance, I could see the silhouette of his round body and round face behind round wire-rim glasses that always seemed to hold the reflection from the one lamp in the room. I couldn't see his eyes, but I was always aware of his pointed Dracula-like canine teeth as he hissed out question after question.

Then one day came his summation based on the culmination of years of study and working with children, "When the boys at school change your last name from Mahan to Gayhan, just say," he lisped and gestured with a limp wrist, "'Shut up, I'm looking for my purse.'"

And thus began my lifelong intrapersonal introspection.

My best friends were food and television. There I could escape from the daily dose of teasing and bullying that I received at the hands of my brothers and kids at school. Even in the face of the nearly constant barrage of belittlement and diminishment, I can see now how I was imprisoned within Stockholm Syndrome and felt the desire to befriend my captors. I did whatever I could do to be who I was expected to be, and I learned to hide what I thought made me different.

It was evident that it was in my best interest to be who my mother needed and wanted me to be when I was around her and then transform into the boy my father hoped for me to be when I was around him. It never seemed to work with my brothers and me as hard as I tried. They simply didn't like me, and we were archenemies. As a survival strategy, I had to become a chameleon with a superhero power that enabled me to disappear.

Needless to say, groups were always tricky for me. School was a daily nightmare. How could I possibly present 25 to 30 different personalities at once in the same room? I couldn't be everyone they wanted me to be and didn't have any idea who I was, so instead, I would simply fade away. I was safe when I was Mr. Cellophane Man. It worked for me.

I remember watching a Woody Allen film, long before I had any idea who he was, the black-and-white mockumentary, *Zelig*, about a man who transformed into whoever he was around, even morphing into having almond-shaped eyes when in the company of Asians. I thought I was watching a documentary. I recall feeling that there were other people out there like me for the first time.

By all appearances, I was cool, aloof, and laid back, but I was seething in anger, self-loathing, and hopelessness underneath it all. I was on an emotional roller coaster that I just couldn't seem to get off. I swung between a quiet rage that I could only express as sarcasm, silent screams into my pillow at night, and a sadness I hid behind the camouflage of cold, lifeless eyes and a monotone whisper voice.

As I grew older, and yet well before the legal age, I expanded my circle of friends to include nicotine, alcohol, and marijuana. They became my gateway drugs into unhealthy relationships, but that was somehow better than the devastation of isolation. They were the common denominator that built the bridge between the island I had become and the opportunity to belong. But even hanging out with 'the cool kids' couldn't help me shake the deep internal knowing that I was intrinsically different.

Miraculously, I did manage to excel academically and artistically. However, by the time I was 14, I had had enough. The bullying I had endured had just about broken me. I passionately campaigned for my parents to send me to boarding school.

What kind of child asks to be sent away to boarding school?

I had hoped that it would be a fresh start. Perhaps there, I could spread my wings a bit and be more of who I was meant to be.

I think, on some level, my mother took it as a personal affront. My father made it crystal clear that I was becoming an even greater expense. If he sent me to boarding school, he would not be able to buy the 1955 Thunderbird convertible that he wanted as a second car. But, to their credit, they were able to see how much pain I was in and let me go. They were also aware of how much pain they would be in if I remained at home.

It was an idyllic enclave tucked away on a mountaintop in Vermont that had been co-ed since 1935, replete with a pond that we called 'the puddle,' a place for the entire student body, faculty, and staff to go skinny dipping. We addressed the headmaster and teachers by their first names—quite the departure from my strict Southern 'Yes, Ma'am, Yes, Sir' upbringing. Studying the arts carried as much weight as academics, and our tests and papers were not given traditional grades but written evaluations instead.

And yet, this began my journey of discovering that no matter where I went, I was there. The school didn't solve my problems, and I managed to get myself suspended from the most progressive boarding school in America. Needless to say, my parents did not allow me to return.

I ended up back at home in Virginia attending Norfolk Catholic High School, and we weren't Catholic. When told on the first day of assembly to sit with my parish, I didn't know what a parish was nor, once again, where I belonged. It turns out that it was in the back left-hand corner of the auditorium, where the non-Catholics gathered. Feeling like I was on the outside looking in was as comfortable and familiar as my favorite jeans with the raggedy holes in the knees dripping white threads tangled in the dryer.

One day when the entire school gathered en masse in the local church for mass, the priest was walking down the aisle, flicking holy water from a laurel branch onto the parishioners. As his arm recoiled in preparation for the absolution of my row, the fear of God sent me scrambling over the back of the pew, afraid that the holy water would blister my skin upon contact. Therein ensued a difficult conversation with the school principal. She seemed just as uncomfortable as Sister Jean was that day in Death and Dying class when I raised my hand.

After a long, deep breath to compose herself, she asked the local heathen, "What, Brian?"

"Sister Jean," I wondered, "What will you do if you die and nothing happens?"

She slammed her Bible shut as if to keep my heretic words from entering her sacred scrolls and paused while staring me down like a chicken in the henhouse trying to protect her eggs from a cold human hand.

"Well, Brian." She exhaled. "I'd probably feel like the biggest fool on the face of the Earth."

She opened her Bible again and proceeded with class. I wasn't trying to question her faith. I seriously needed an answer.

Eventually, and much to my parents' discomfiture, I auditioned against 1,500 young hopefuls. I was accepted into the class of 30 students at one of the best schools in the country to study 'the craft,' North Carolina School of the Arts.

I had always acted. I was bitten by the bug in grade school. I remember the first time I made an audience laugh. Everything changed in that split second.

Acting, I realized, allowed me to retire my cloak of invisibility and leverage my chameleon skills. If I weren't in a school play, I was in a local community production. My first review in the local paper by a bitter critic renowned for his sharp tongue filled me with determination. He said that I had 'promise.'

But at the end of my first year, I was called into the office of my acting teacher. Little did I know that I was about to get schooled.

In his deep, resonating, theatrical voice, he started and end-ed the brief conversation the moment my butt hit the chair. "Brian, the theater has all too long been a haven for neurotics. And I think it's time it stopped."

He then slid me the business card of a psychotherapist across his polluted desk. I took the card in silence and left.

I called the number and made an appointment. At first, we talked about my social anxiety. Over time, as we continued spiraling deeper into my abyss, my therapist explained that she thought I was having a midlife crisis at 19. (But I couldn't afford a shiny new red sports car.) She said I was dealing with things that most men pushed off until their 40s. I guess I was just a gross overachiever and ahead of my time.

After leaving school, I made the perfunctory move to The Great White Way in the Big Apple with a brief pit stop into psychoanalysis. I mean, it was the '80s in New York City, and everybody was doing it. But I wanted direction and answers, which apparently was not what my analyst was willing to im-part. Session after session, I lay on a worn pleather fainting couch, answering, once again, question after question. She never made a statement. And I wanted answers. One day, I was so frustrated by the process I decided that I wouldn't an-swer any more questions. And so she sat there and waited for my response. And I lay there stonewalling for several minutes in silence.

Eventually, she leaned forward and whispered, "Where are you?"

To which I replied, "If you can't tell I'm right here in the room with you, then there certainly isn't any reason for me being here."

I collected my belongings and what was left of my psyche and walked out.

One day not too long afterward, I stumbled upon two books in the window display of an old bookstore in Manhattan. The bell above the door rang when I entered and found a dusty old man crouched over an old dusty desk, lost in an old dusty book. Like a Pavlovian response, he startled and tried to look at me as I walked in. But he had been hunched over books for so long his body held the same crooked posture and moved like one unit stuck in time and space. I purchased Shirley MacLaine's *Out on a Limb* and Louise Hay's *You Can Heal Your Life*. Combined, both titles regaled my internal battles. And in short order, they changed the way that I saw the world and myself.

That was when I began to read nearly as voraciously as my father did. The most predominant memories of my father from my early childhood were of me peering through the gap in the pocket doors of his library as he lay on the couch reading. Consequently, I had mixed feelings about books. And now I also had mixed drinks about my feelings.

Like many actors before me, I paid my dues by waiting tables and attending master classes. I did some work on the Soap Operas, *The Guiding Light* and *As the World Turns*—only now do I see the irony. I also performed in student and indie films and starred in a few off-off-off Broadway shows. My agent called me 'The King of Callbacks,' as I frequently got to the final meeting with producers and then did not get the part. One such meeting eventually landed me in Hollywood, California. I flew from NYC to LA for my final meeting to replace Johnny Depp on the hit TV series *21 Jump Street.*

I blew every big shot I got. I could never understand why I always choked, but it was my undeniable pattern. Cognitive dissonance won out, once again. I had the mental conviction that being a classically trained actor, I was the better choice over Richard Grieco, but I also carried the embodied belief that I didn't deserve it.

Internalized toxic shame was my constant companion and a highly skilled saboteur.

Since I had gotten fired from just about every restaurant short-sighted enough to hire me to wait tables in NYC, I decided to remain in LA and become a massage therapist. It was the perfect job for me. I only had to exchange initial pleasantries, and the rest of the time was spent in silence. And I enjoyed it; it allowed me several hours a day of moving meditation.

Plus, I could arrange my clients around my auditions, rehearsals, and performances. I wrote, produced, and performed a one-man show in Hollywood that proved my first critic right. This time, the reviews that came in were so good people thought I had made them up:

" . . . strong enough to shine and dazzle even in the dark."
(A command performance of my foray into therapy.)

"You will never consider his hour upon the stage *Time Lost* [the title of the show]."
(And the story of my life.)

"[He] achieves magic."
(And can make himself disappear.)

But I had an inner critic, too. And he ruled my world.

His voice had become so loud and debilitating that I determined it was time to gag him with Prozac. The doctor told me that it could take up to three weeks before I would notice a difference. I didn't want to waste a moment and tossed the first pill into the back of my mouth and swallowed it dry. As my convertible transported the soon-to-be old me with the wind in my hair on the I-10 freeway, the strangest feeling came over me. The lead suit I had been wearing my whole life, unbeknownst to me, began to lift away, and I watched it in the rearview mirror flip around like a plastic shopping bag across the highway of life. I felt light as a feather, and my negative cyclical thinking faded away, much like I had for so many years. I began to cry. For the first time, I felt normal.

My wanderlust for greener pastures continued. At last count, I have lived in Thirty-nine different abodes, the longest being most recently in the same house for 15 years. I'm now 57. Do the math. Thirty-nine places in 41 years to hang my head—er, I mean, my hat.

I was the six-foot-three wallflower, always standing in a differ-ent corner of the world. But slowly—really, really slowly, year by year—I actually seemed to make some strides. I even made a few friends along the way. And I didn't burn them out and had them running for the hills as quickly as I once did. Grant-ed, my friends were all like characters out of Santa's Land for Broken Toys. They would joke that they had to hold a mirror in front of me—to see if I was still breathing.

One time, I expressed how excited I was about something, and a friend quipped, "Oh yeah? Tell that to your face."

But when it came to matters of the heart, when I surrendered into intimacy and could trust enough to feel my feelings and share them transparently with another, I put my vulnerable Self at risk. When I fell in love, I fell hard. I lost the boundary between me and the other. I thought the whole idea was to merge and become one. I would sacrifice my Self: my needs, my desires, my voice, my goals, and my dreams to become, once again, what I believed my partner needed and wanted me to be.

So at the time, it seemed like a nervous breakdown, only now I know that it was a nervous *breakthrough*.

My resting bitch face had shattered. Some might have called it a countenance of consternation or a face that, even when at rest, could not belie the journey of a thousand miles that began even before my first step. A squinched and pinched screeching visage had resurfaced. The sour contortion of my face felt undeniably old and familiar, an embodied memory of having been left alone as a child and untouched for entirely too long. Not that that had been the norm, but often enough.

But this time, my heart had been broken. Again. And instead of it getting more manageable over the years, with each cycle of falling in love followed by subsequent ruthless abandonment, the grief had compounded exponentially. I hadn't toughened up over time; I had developed thin skin.

The floodgates had finally given way to the pressure from the long-held, and no-longer-containable, wellspring of despair and futility. My body heaved convulsively as if it were trying to break itself in two, as I sobbed and sobbed inconsolably for days on end. My abs were so spent from weeping that I could barely sit up, and I had shed so many tears I had become dehydrated.

I remember telling a friend of mine, "If a gallon of water weighs eight pounds, then I should be back to my birth weight by now!"

On this particular night, I lay on the floor in the dark hallway of my apartment with the telephone beside me. Desperately seeking solace from whoever might happen to answer the call, I worked my way down the speed-dial list of unsuspecting friends, struggling through my tears to read the next name on the list.

It was a time when people still answered their phones, but apparently, no one was at home on the west coast. However, on the east coast, my mother did what all mothers do when the phone rings in the middle of the night: she picked up the phone, assuming the worst.

But my banshee shriek was unrecognizable even to her. Her voice broke with confusion and concern.

"Who is this?" she screamed back. "*Who is this*?!"

"It's your son. It's your son, Brian!" I said through my sobs, realizing that I needed to clarify which of the three of us it was.

I grew up thinking my name was Je-Gre-Brian, because she would often start to call me by my oldest brother Jeff's name, then catch herself and default to using my middle brother Greg's name before landing on mine. Again, that was not the norm, but it happened often enough.

Beyond that, I can't recall our conversation, nor how I ended up fully dressed in the empty bathtub. But I could have filled it with my own tears. The sound coming out of me ricocheted off porcelain and amplified off tile and must have been unlike anything the neighbors had ever heard before. I recalled that when I was growing up, we weren't allowed to yell in the house because the neighbors might hear. This time was different. I didn't care. Perhaps I was even hoping that a stranger would come to my emotional rescue.

In fact, sometime later, I discovered that the upstairs neighbor in my duplex had been at home and listened to my cries all night but chose not to come down to help me. Perhaps he had already grown accustomed to, and weary of, the sounds of my sorrow wafting up through his floorboards.

Although Mom told me that she would be on the next plane out to help me pick up the pieces of me, in my mind, it wasn't enough. I needed someone, anyone, there for me now. Like an infant's distress builds over time from moans of discomfort from being cold and wet into wails of despair, now terrified that the ultimate instinctual fear has been realized: abandonment.

After Mom hung up to prepare for the flight, my fingers continued their journey down the speed-dial list. At last, a couple—new friends of mine, who I had fortuitously added to my speed dial just a few days before—answered their phone. They eventually had to break into my house because I couldn't pull myself out of the tub to answer the door. Ill-equipped to pack my stuffing back inside of me, they put me into a taxi and instructed the driver to take me to the emergency room, where I was unceremoniously strapped down like an animal to a gurney 'for my own protection.'

But it did not seem like a safe place. I couldn't ignore the stench of blood, vomit, and bleach. The din of chaos reverberated throughout the halls. Had I not been restrained, I would have been flopping around in horror like a fish on a hot rock.

How had I gone from the privileges of being a doctor's kid to being an uninsured man at Los Angeles County Hospital?

Hours passed, and eventually, a kind, thin man in a white lab coat approached me. He introduced himself as he touched my shoulder and explained my options.

He told me he could admit me into the nutter ward, where, he warned, "You will see things that you can never unsee."

He reflexively swiped his glasses off his face and rubbed his eyes as if he could cleanse away the images of his day-to-day life. I thought to myself if this is what the hallways were like, I couldn't even imagine what awaited me behind closed doors.

On a long, slow exhale, he offered me a way out. "Or, if you promise me that you won't hurt yourself, you can go home if you have a friend come and pick you up."

I chose the latter.

In the mid-'90s, one of my friends offered for me to come to Maui, Hawaii, to care for his dog while he left to visit his family on the mainland. I jumped at the chance to have some R&R, but not without making it a deeply personal mission. It was to be a spiritual quest. I packed 12 years of journals into their own suitcase and headed to 'The Rock.' It was not the first or last time I would seek refuge on the world's most remote land-mass. I was excited to have time to contemplate my navel and read about all of the progress that I had made over the years.

Once I settled into my board shorts and flip-flops, I made my way to where the salty air of the tropical wind blew the waves and my hair back. I plopped an armful of tattered journals and myself down onto the hot white sand and began to read and read. Page after page, I was sickened to discover that I was reading the same thing over and over and over. I hadn't changed. I hadn't evolved. I hadn't learned, and I hadn't grown. I still battled with all of the same ol' shit. I was gutted.

How could that be? Was I hardwired into patterns and vicious cycles of repetition? Was this my fate—a life of struggle and mediocrity? A massive blanket of shame smothered me. Why was it that mantras, *The Secret*, affirmations, *The Law of Attraction*, vision boards, and creative visualizations worked for others, but not for me?

I reached for my Life Alert button; I was crestfallen and I couldn't get up.

So I quit reading. In fact, in that moment of clarity, I quit everything. No more six days a week of yoga, no more trying to pray it away, no more diligent enforcement of new positive thoughts.

I was done, done, and done!

From here on out, I decided that I would adopt the Buddhist principle of 'chop wood; carry water.' I was going to simply be an animal on the planet, just a squirrel looking for a nut. The days bled into weeks as the months melted into years. And I didn't care. About anything. I even began to give up on my dream of being an actor. I was resolved to be a complex man living a simple life.

Why Read This Book?

Why I Write

Psychotropic medication numbed me out, which initially felt like relief and freedom. But eventually, it became clear that it kept me stuck in place, unable to access what needed to heal. Consequently, I couldn't change or grow.

Traditional talk therapy seemed to make things worse the more I repeated telling my stories. Granted, it helped to challenge some perspectives that I had held and reframe some of my maladaptive thinking, but, ultimately, it left me feeling as if I were unfixable—especially when old patterns continued to be perpetuated and self-loathing refused to recede.

The benefits that I gleaned from spiritual and physical practices were life-changing in many ways, yet not enough to manifest profound and long-lasting change. Over time, I had created a daisy chain of activities that would commence before I even opened my eyes in the morning. I began each day contemplating the gratitude that I could muster, beginning with the awareness of the loft, of my mattress, and the comforting weight and texture of my linens.

My morning ritual continued until noon. I spent most of my time like a tiger chasing its tail, one practice after the next to stave off the feelings of despair and negative cyclical thoughts that plagued me. The Serenity Prayer, 'God, grant me the serenity to accept the things I cannot change, the courage to change the things I can, and the wisdom to know the difference,' was my version of the Buddhist chant, 'Nam Myoho Renge Kyo,' and repeated on an endless loop in my mind.

I've always been the type of person that has wanted to improve the quality of my life. And whenever I found anything that brought me any relief or benefit whatsoever, I felt compelled to shout it from the rooftop. I had an irrepressible compulsion to tell my friends about a good book I was reading, supplements I found to be effective, a more efficient way to work out, or a funny video that could bring a smile to someone's face.

Despite all my struggles, when looking back on my life, I see how I had always been, for my friends, an ear, the hand to hold, the eyes to bear witness, the heart to feel one's own reflection, a shoulder to lean on, or a leg up. My own pain and torment provided the common ground for empathy. Sympathy created a sense of connectivity within commiseration. And my tender-hearted compassion became a reliable soft spot to land.

I even built and ran a lifestyle management company for 12 years called Enlightened Concierge. I helped my clients find the very best personal trainers, chefs, massage therapists, Reiki masters, feng shui consultants, and dozens of other services that would improve their quality of life.

My clients kept wanting to try different practitioners and more and more services because they weren't ultimately feeling better. Four different massage therapists, three chiropractors, and two acupuncturists couldn't fix their chronic tension. A feng shui consultant, three yogis teaching various styles, a meditation teacher, and a professional organizer weren't enough to calm their anxiety and bring an inner sense of peace or relaxation. A life coach, a private chef, and a nutritionist, working together, still couldn't break their pattern of self-sabotage and weight gain.

And even though I was able to provide for myself and my clients a healthier lifestyle, I noticed that it wasn't enough. Unwittingly, I had built a business focused on managing and mitigating people's symptoms. We were all still ignoring the root causes of all our pain.

I'm frustrated by most people's misunderstandings and misconceptions about stress, trauma, and shame. In my humble opinion, based on my own complete reversal of PTSD and my clinical experience treating clients for more than 17 years, when trauma is properly understood and worked with the way that it needs to be, healing is nearly certain.

In December 2003, my doctor wrote the four letters PTSD in my chart. (And my health insurance company promptly canceled my policy.) In January of 2004, a month after my car wreck, Dr. Connie suggested I begin seeing a Somatic Experiencing practitioner. After three sessions, my panic attacks stopped entirely. And I haven't had a panic attack in over 17 years.

I couldn't wrap my mind around how quickly things turned around for me. Somatic Experiencing worked far better than all of the other symptom-addressing techniques combined. I had to figure out what happened and how I could share it with others. Within two weeks of that third session, I began training to become a practitioner. Even though my presenting symptoms had resolved, I continued to do the inner-work because I kept feeling better and getting better.

And I've had more than 25 clients over the years who have had a similar experience and subsequently took the three-year training and got certified, as well. I think that is a pretty profound testament to the technique's efficacy. Trauma can be a teacher and a tool. Consequently, I believe in post-traumatic growth.

Several years ago, I began creating dozens of informational videos and posting them on YouTube. That led to my first international client and, eventually, my international clientele. I created and held my own workshops and retreats. I accepted every opportunity to speak in front of small groups and all invitations to be interviewed by anyone with a larger platform. For many years, I assisted in and taught trainings for mental health professionals, thinking that by doing so, they would then take the information and skills that they learned into their practices, and, indirectly, I would be helping even more people. During the initial throes and woes of COVID, I gratefully sustained a triple private practice of 48 clients per week. I'm also working on creating live and evergreen online trainings, one of which will be the companion piece for this book.

Never in a million years would I ever have imagined that I would end up doing what I do. It was undeniably a stroke of fate from the strike of one bumper on another that turned my world upside down so that it could ultimately be uprighted and reoriented. As untethered as I seemingly was, I look back now and see that there never really was a single misstep. I simply could not have gotten to where I am without having been so lost for so long.

And now, my life's mission is to help one million people properly heal from trauma. To mix my metaphors, that makes me feel like Sisyphus pretending to be Hercules while rolling planet Earth onto the broad shoulders of Atlas. I'm hoping this book will have the ripple effect of scalability and will continue to further my reach.

I hope you will share this book with everyone you think may benefit from reading it. Books need to go viral more than cat videos or different people dancing to the same 15 seconds of a song.

The Secret Sauce

*M*y aspiration for you is that this book will help you fast-track your healing process, regardless of where you may be on your journey. Perhaps you are fortunate enough to find this book at the outset of your search, and it may become the primer for you, like *Out on a Limb* and *You Can Heal Your Life* were for me. Or you may be a seasoned seeker who is primed and ready to quit carrying out the same thoughts, words, and actions, expecting different results, and courageously redirect your attention to your original wounds.

My intent is to help you build a strong foundation of knowledge and understanding about what trauma and the trauma of shame are. From that vantage point, I am sure that you will be able to see how early events in your life created many of the beliefs that you still hold about yourself, the people in your life, the world around you, and the ways in which you currently engage with the world. I want to help you realize how the beliefs you formed at times in your life when you had limited intellect, life experience, resources, and support continue to influence you in ways that you may not attribute to these early wounding experiences. I am determined to help you discover that there are effective ways to free yourself from old limiting beliefs, even when they are unconscious, so that you don't continue the patterns of thinking and behaving that will create a future that is a near carbon copy of your past.

Yes, these are lofty goals, but achieving them is quite doable.

Sometimes we must forget what we know and return to basics. I want to keep this book and your process short and simple. This book is not meant to be a deep dive, or a place of extensive scientific reference, because I don't want you to have to sort through information that scientifically and conceptually supports what I am saying but doesn't move the needle for you. This is written to be easily comprehended, a layperson's guide to healing trauma and the trauma of shame. I will leave the research to the neuroscientists and to your Google searches. (And stop with the Google searches. You are driving yourself bonkers.)

That said, however, there is one fascinating and groundbreaking 20-year-long study conducted at the University of Chicago by Dr. Eugene Gendlin that I think will help put things into a clear perspective for you. Dr. Gendlin hoped to clarify the factors that influence a positive outcome in the therapeutic process. Essentially, he set out to answer the question: why did some patients get better while others did not?

His life's work led to the advent of the body-mind connection in the therapeutic process. Using his findings, he wrote the books *The Felt Sense* and *Focusing,* which has sold 500,000 copies in 17 languages. He was a four-time honoree of the American Psychological Association, including the first to receive a Distinguished Professional Award in Psychology and Psychotherapy. And he received a lifetime achievement award from the United States Association for Body Psychotherapy. He also founded the journal Psychotherapy: *Theory, Research and Practice.*

His empirical research explored all the different types of therapy: Freudian, Jungian, gestalt, psychoanalysis, cognitive behavioral therapy, etc. He also studied the therapists themselves. How did their ability to establish rapport and create a sense of safety for the client affect the therapeutic process? And how did the therapists' abilities to skillfully apply tools and techniques impact their case studies' transformation?

Of course, he found that the type of therapy needed to be congruent with the clients' issues and that the therapeutic alliance established between therapist and client is paramount. But he also discovered something entirely unexpected.

Drum roll, please!

The single most determining factor as to whether or not any-one gets better in any practice with any practitioner is based on the patients' innate capacities to feel sensations in their bodies, language those sensations appropriately, and then connect them with the correct emotion and attach the right meaning.

So allow me to detail this out for you.

Following traumatic events, there is often a breakdown in communication within different areas of the brain. Imagine an automobile accident or a stalled car blocking the number-two lane on a freeway. Traffic no longer flows freely in that lane, and the other lanes become congested, too. The information that normally flows in that lane can no longer do so freely. Until the physiological obstruction in the number-two lane is towed away, the wound continues to fester and will undoubt-edly continue to get triggered over time and resurface. And when that obstruction is still in place, there is a strong likeli-hood that it will cause another collision, adding to the chaos. This disorganization can affect thoughts, language, and criti-cal thinking but how we process emotion, social engagement, memory, and the freeze-flight-fight survival strategy.

So, according to Gendlin's findings, there is a fundamental missing link in some therapeutic approaches. Talking about your problems or past events isn't enough, nor is reconceptu-alizing the experience. Catharsis, releasing repressed emotion, may be helpful, but it may not be a true healing experience, even though there may be a temporary sense of relief from internal emotional pressure.

Gendlin's research confirms that it is imperative to explore the sensations that comprise emotions by leaning into them with curiosity. In doing so, our interpretation of what we are feeling might change, and we can then identify and address them more correctly. We must inquire about how we are conceptualizing the cluster of sensations we are experiencing, as well as the meanings or beliefs that we have formed about both the individual sensations and the emotional expression.

When the body talks, it does so through sensations. A sensation is an uncomplicated, finite, expressive communication to you from your nervous system. It's the body's way of saying, "Hey, you! Yes, you! Pay attention! Over here, over here!"

You want to know when a spider is crawling up your leg, right? You understand the gravity of not being able to discern hot from scalding.

The most essential part of any communication process is listening. Your body is sending a message, but you need to be open to listening to that message. Sensations seek out our attention, and we listen to that communication from our nervous system by intentionally directing our attention to these sensations. Deliberately feeling the sensations that we have in our bodies allows us to listen to the messages they are trying to tell us.

However, a single sensation can be difficult to zero in on. Our minds gravitate toward complexity and underestimate the value of a singular sensation, so we may, therefore, disregard it altogether. There is also a lot of room for misinterpreting sensations. For instance, many people mistake the sensation of thirst for hunger and they will eat instead of drink.

On top of that, most people immediately begin trying to change whatever they are feeling at first blush. When they start to feel cold, they put on a sweater. A few minutes later, they begin to feel warm, so they take the sweater off. Our tolerance for feeling anything has become nearly nonexistent. It's as if our higher brain thinks that if we feel anything, something is wrong.

As well, bodily sensations and their respective emotions can be confusing. A client of mine was flabbergasted to discover that she had been mistaking anxiety for hunger for years. Anytime her mind would race about current or future challenges, she would feel in her belly some of the more pronounced sensations of anxiety and, unwittingly, self-soothe with food because she thought that she was hungry.

From a neurobiological perspective, an emotion is the umbrella experience of a collection of sensations in various areas of the body, co-occurring with the presence of neurochemicals, like endorphins, cortisol, adrenaline, dopamine, serotonin, oxytocin, etc., combined with micro-movements or gross behaviors.

The primary emotions, anger, sadness, fear, joy, curiosity, surprise, disgust, and shame, are all multidimensional. And each of the hundreds of shades of gray of primary emotions, referred to as affects, have their own unique expressions.

Emotions can be overwhelming, full-body experiences for children, and the adults in the room rarely know how to hold the space for their children's emotions. Due to our socialization around emotions, we often hold strong beliefs that it is not okay to have them and that it is unsafe to express them.

This learned resistance to feeling is generally the most uncomfortable part of whatever it is we are currently feeling. I don't like it; I don't want to feel it; I want it to go away; it is scary or painful. For example, the sensation of an itch is met with a disproportionate reaction to make it go away by scratching it.

But when we can move willingly into curiosity, we collapse the resistance, and often we find that what we are truly feeling, a tiny little tickle, is much more tolerable than we thought. And we can also learn, as adults, how to do that with our emotions.

My definition of intolerable is that it's time to go to the emergency room. So until that threshold is reached, it's manageable. When I realize that, in that moment, I step into empowerment. It may suck rocks, but I am able to be present with this feeling. Becoming amenable to feeling what I am feeling and focusing my conscious awareness on the sensations that are occurring allows my emotions to naturally and organically resolve themselves.

For instance, we may have learned that expressing anger hurts others or is met with retaliation. Boys are taught that they need to stick up for themselves and given a bit more freedom to have and express anger, but for girls, doing so is 'unladylike.' Sadness is a sign of weakness for boys because 'big boys don't cry,' but girls are comforted and receive sympathy and empathy when they cry. This mixed message can result in a conflation of anger and sadness. Men tend to become enraged when what they are actually feeling is hurt and vulnerable, while women are more likely to cry when what they are really feeling, underneath the tears, is pissed off or frustrated.

Of course, I'm speaking in generalities, as this phenomenon is not exclusively gendered. I can't tell you how many times over the past 17-plus years I have had both men and women sobbing in front of me, but the words that come out of their mouths are, "I'm so angry."

Here is another example of how important it is to fully understand the difference between sensations and emotions. Anxiety and excitement are nearly identical in their presentation. I'll say that again: Anxiety and excitement are nearly identical in their presentation. But, how could that be? It is an almost perfect example of the polarization of opposites. One signals the need for retreat, and the other compels us to move forward. Regardless, both are identified by the same bodily behaviors and sensations: elevated heart rate, short and shallow breathing, trembling and shaking, change in body temperature, clammy hands, and, in extreme cases, tunnel vision.

I have seen clients who mistook anxiety for excitement and moved toward danger and others who mistook excitement for anxiety and moved away from potentially exhilarating and rewarding experiences. This is why Dr. Gendlin specified the importance of attaching the right affect (emotion) to the collection of correctly named sensations and the need to then attach the right meaning or beliefs.

Often, when I ask a client what they currently feel in their body, they will tell me what they have noticed historically, like anxiety, panic, or emptiness, but specify that they don't feel that right now. Alternatively, they may say that they feel sad, depressed, or anxious. Some will report back that they don't really feel anything. Rarely does a new client present with clear and specific use of sensation words.

Whatever an individual's state of awareness may be, it is their starting point for the process to commence. Miraculous things begin to happen when these foundational elements are woven into any therapeutic practice. Unequivocally, they must be an integral part of the healing process, especially and specifically when working with trauma and the trauma of shame. Once again, trauma is a physiological wound that needs to be addressed physiologically in order to fully heal.

For many highly intelligent people, the body is merely a vehicle to move their head through space. What matters most to them is their thoughts, goals, and achievements. Overthinkers have a propensity to be under feelers. Even if they acknowledge they are feeling an emotion and don't tune it out right away, the mind can often trivialize the emotion and, instead, prioritize focus on the meaning or belief about the emotion. They seem to consciously diminish the body's communication as irrelevant. After all, they believe that if they feel something, something is wrong, and if they feel nothing, everything is okay. They may find greater enjoyment in intellectual discourse than sexual intercourse.

For others, a lifetime of pain and discomfort has turned their body into a house of horrors. No wonder they don't want to feel. As a defense against their ever-present inner turmoil, they develop highly effective ways to dissociate, disconnect, or distract themselves.

Years ago, I sat with a client, a buttoned-up, stiff-upper-lip kind of guy. If there were a rule as to how many designers one could wear at the same time, he clearly wasn't aware of it—and his clothes practically looked painted on. He had that kind of body that is only possible if you have entirely too much free time on your hands. The strain that his muscles put on the seams of his clothing created palpable tension in the room— like if one seam were to give way and begin to unravel, he would, too.

"I've never had a girlfriend," he divulged. He had come to see me because he wanted reassurance that there wasn't anything wrong with that.

"Never?" He caught me off guard.

"I don't buy into stereotypical relationships. In fact, most people kind of bore me," he said.

I wasn't sure if he was trying to convince himself or me.

"I'm fine," he insisted. "I like my independence, and I love my alone time. It's just who I am."

Rolling his eyes and adjusting the 25-pound gold watch on his wrist, he said flatly, "I had a charmed and idyllic childhood with loving and attentive parents . . . I mean, they divorced when I was like three, I think, but I was too young to really remember any of it." He closed his eyes, and his thoughts began to slow down, as did his delivery. "And . . . I actually . . . kinda liked . . . having two homes and two . . . two sets of toys and clothes and everything. They . . . really did their best . . . to be good parents."

"I'm curious," I said. "What, if anything, did you notice happening in your body when you shared that with me?"

He reported back to me that his stomach felt weird, but it was probably because he had just eaten. And his shoulders were really tight, but he was convinced that that was from working out. But my sense was that neither had to do with what he had eaten or his workouts. I discovered that he always rationalized what it was or why he was feeling it.

I encouraged him to simply be an empathetic witness to the weird feeling in his stomach without needing to rationalize why it was there—to simply lean in with curiosity.

"Let's see what, if anything, might happen if you were to allow your awareness to explore the real estate that that weird feeling takes up in your stomach."

Before I could finish my thought, I watched his back arch as his neck twisted. His chest expanded, and the space between the buttons on his shirt opened wide enough to expose flesh. For quite some time, he did not exhale. I could see his eyes darting back and forth behind his fluttering eyelids.

Then, a solitary tear crested the cage of lashes, making a break for it down his cheek. But its flash-in-the-pan moment of freedom was dashed with the impulsive grazing of the back of his hand as if using his fingertips would have made it too obvious what he was doing.

"Well, I wasn't expecting that." He chuckled, adjusting himself in the chair.

With a gentle tilt of my head, I asked, "What happened?"

"It was nothing really. Probably some kind of . . ." Unable to complete his own sentence, he flailed his arms and hands about a bit as if he could erase the image. "I don't know. Like some kind of . . . phantom memory . . . but obviously not a memory because I can't actually fly . . . or, I mean float." He shook his head, trying to dismiss the image. "I was looking down at myself? In the box. Besides, it doesn't make any sense." His tone sounded final until he blurted out, "I was see-ing me . . . I mean, how could I see me looking at me? Like I was in three places at once or something. I don't know, dude. That was just Looney Tunes."

He sat in silence for several moments, looking directly into my eyes. I held his gaze without discomfort or expectation. I wit-nessed subtle emotion wash over him wave after wave. We felt safe together, and neither one of us felt like we needed to fill the silence. His thoughts slowly began to organize, and when he was ready, he told me that he had been in an incuba-tor for several weeks as an infant.

As things continued to unwind, we discovered together that his birth experience and the period of time leading up to his parents' divorce created beliefs within him that people couldn't be trusted to meet his needs. He had learned he was better off figuring out how to be the source of his own happiness.

He didn't have explicit memories of his birth experience or of his parents fighting, but clearly, the implicit memories of his early developmental traumas continued to influence him. Apparently, his explicit memories changed over time as he re-framed the neglect and abandonment.

So, just because you can't remember an event doesn't mean that it isn't still held in the body and can't get triggered and re-surface. And, just because you may think that you have made peace with specific past experiences, it doesn't mean that they don't still affect you and influence the trajectory of your life. Finally, just because you don't know what you're feeling doesn't mean you're not feeling it.

The Nitty-Gritty

*M*y job is to get my clients to quit seeing me as quickly as possible. To do so, I must help my clients increase their capacity to feel what they are feeling and to report back to me in clear language what they have become aware of in their bodies. Then, together, we can explore the meaning and beliefs that they have about their bodily sensations and the expression of their emotions.

I am a 'basics and fundamentals' kind of guy. I like clean food, streamlined systems, a detailed calendar, things that are time-tested and proven, and the shortest, fastest, most effective way of doing things. This has all led me to understand this simple truth: you need to stop chasing down symptoms and start focusing on the root causes, which are trauma and the trauma of shame.

You may not think that you are traumatized or have shame. You may not be aware of the intricacies and long-term implications of trauma and shame. You might not even fully understand what either really is, but that doesn't mean that they don't still impact and influence your life.

Trauma is often misunderstood, misdiagnosed, undiagnosed, or underdiagnosed. Trauma is not reserved for veterans of war or victims of abuse. The little 't' traumas, or what I call 'death by a thousand paper cuts,' like the devastation of shame, are often even more dysregulating and multifarious than big 'T' Traumas.

You may be surprised to learn that many of your current day-to-day challenges are, more than likely, symptomatic reenactments of past traumatic events. Even if you can't recall bad things happening to you, you still may very well be suffering due to unresolved past traumatic events.

For many reasons, you might not have the conscious memory in the form of visual images that you can recall now in the present moment. Memories are malleable and suppressible. Just because you remember something a certain way doesn't mean that that is the way it actually occurred. Your memory of an event can be influenced over time by other people's accounts of the same event. Plus, just because you don't remember something doesn't mean that it didn't happen or that it doesn't still affect you. You can be traumatized when you are preverbal, precognitive, preconceptual, and before you have the capacity for explicit memory.

The neurobiological mechanics of lucid memory don't begin to come online physiologically until about 18 to 24 months. Because of this, many medical procedures on infants, like circumcision, continue to be conducted without anesthesia since the child won't have any cognitive memory of it. And then it takes time for that system to develop and to become more dependable, but it ultimately is never 100 percent reliable—except for the rare cases of people like the actress Marilu Henner from the TV series *Taxi*. Henner can remember every single moment of her life, including what she ate for each meal, what shoes she wore, and which day of the week it was, regardless of how long ago the occasion.

Over time, most of us develop the ability to search the recesses of our minds for specific memories, like looking for a particular file in a filing cabinet. However, we have all had the experience of racking our minds to try to remember something that we just can't seem to recall. These types of memories are called explicit memories—and sometimes, a bit of a misnomer, 'long-term memory.'

You also have implicit memory or body memory. These consist of kinesthetic imprints that exist before explicit memory is possible. Infants need to recall what causes them pain and discomfort and what garners them the kind of attention they need for survival. The body remembers. It has to in order to ensure its own survival. In general, memory is highly influenced by emotional states and stress, which is why you have a tendency to remember extraordinary moments, much more so than what you had for lunch last Thursday.

Just like an emotion is a collection of sensations, so are implicit memories in the body. Implicit memories can be triggered by things that you see, hear, smell, touch, or taste, or by internal stimuli, like a feeling that you are having in your body now that's similar to how you felt at a different time in your life. All these triggers can suddenly flood you with that unexpected memories.

Explicit memories can include implicit memory, but not all implicit memories include explicit memory. Often, early implicit memories seem unanchored in anything tangible other than the sentient experience itself, which can be the case with birth traumas, like having gotten stuck in the birth canal, being delivered with suction cups or forceps, or having had the umbilical cord wrapped around your neck.

Dr. Peter A. Levine, the creator of Somatic Experiencing, says trauma occurs in the body, not in the event or in the mind. Dr. Levine, has received two doctorates—one in psychology from International University and another in medical biophysics from the University of California at Berkeley. In 2010, he received a lifetime achievement award from the United States Association for Body Psychotherapy. He is a member of the American Psychological Association and the International Society for Traumatic Stress Studies. He worked with NASA during the development of the Space Shuttle. He is the creator of Somatic Experiencing and the founder of Somatic Experiencing International. His first book, *Waking the Tiger*, an international bestseller, has been translated into 29 languages, and he has authored and co-authored 8 other books.

Once you fully understand trauma and the trauma of shame, you can begin to address your original wounds in the way in which they are most effectively healed. This will also allow you to examine the defenses and beliefs that you have formed and clung to over time, as well as their roles in keeping you stuck in patterns and vicious cycles. The missing link lies in realizing trauma and the trauma of shame are physiological wounds.

If we can become traumatized when we are preverbal, precognitive, and preconceptual before we can think and reason (a higher brain function), then clearly, another system is at play. That system is the lower brain (primitive brain), which governs the nervous system. The sympathetic nervous system expresses the sentient experience of arousal that we feel when facing a threat of any kind, perceived or real. The autonomic nervous system helps to manage and settle the sympathetic charge after the threat is gone.

Even before your higher brain has the chance to form a thought, you may find yourself screaming or gasping for air, dry-mouthed or sweating, crouching or in a fight stance, running away or immobilized, your heart racing or pounding slowly, trembling and shaking or rigidly frozen. Alternatively, your body could stutter like you have one foot on the gas and the other on the brake.

When we detect danger of any kind, our bodies react. In other words, whether it is an animal baring its teeth or someone giving you a side-eye glance, your brain shifts into its own default defense mode. These defensive actions your body takes are based on specific prior life experiences—or the culmination thereof. Regardless if the threat is perceived, like a side-eye glance, or real, like an animal baring its teeth, your previously learned response kicks in like a knee-jerk reaction. If your learned response is to freeze, then you might be rendered speechless or act like a deer caught in the headlights. But if you have a tendency to flee, you might change the subject or run for your life. If you are stuck in a fight response, you might call out the gesture and volley insults or stick your chest out and step toward the angry dog, gesturing for it to back off.

You might also have an embodied shame response that becomes over-coupled with the event. The terror that you may have fallen out of favor, that it was your fault, or you could have done something differently to have prevented the situation compounds the overall experience.

Your body can react this way even when you witness something horrible happen to someone else—i.e., watching the news and witnessing people dying from COVID and having to say goodbye to their loved ones on an iPad Zoom call. A part of you imagines that it is happening or could happen to you, personally, and in that moment, your lower brain mobilizes your defense responses to freeze, flee, or fight. The perception that you are in danger has become very real because of the ways that your body is now reacting and behaving.

And herein lies the potential for that event to be highly stressful or traumatizing. Simply put, if your nervous system's energetic arousal is able to unwind, discharge, and return to resilience, the event was stressful. If your nervous system's response was unable, for any reason, to complete the process and remains in a state of dysregulation, then the event was traumatic. That is how you have a physiological condition due to trauma, not a psychological disorder.

Granted, over time, you may develop psychological issues, too. This can happen as your mind continues to revisit the experience and tries to make sense of it or to find a way to compartmentalize it. Retelling your story can re-traumatize you because, once again, your reptilian brain is experiencing it as if it is happening all over again. Doing so, repetitively, literally creates a neurological loop, like the needle is stuck in a scratch on a record and is digging the groove deeper and deeper.

Shame, too, is initially (and inherently) a physiological survival mechanism that occurs as a response to a nearly impossible internal crisis: the fear of rejection, abandonment, neglect, or being cast off. These things are on par with the fear of death. Humans are the only species on the planet that are 100 percent dependent upon others for their survival for nearly 25 percent of their lives.

Here are a few more stats to chew on:

According to the US Department of Veterans Affairs, "About 6 out of every 100 people (or 6% of the population) will have PTSD at some point in their lives. About 15 million adults have PTSD during a given year. This is only a small portion of those who have gone through a trauma. About 8 of every 100 women (or 8%) develop PTSD sometime in their lives compared with about 4 of every 100 men (or 4%)."[2]

"Some 88 percent of men and 79 percent of women with PTSD also have another psychiatric disorder. Nearly half suffer from major depression, 16 percent from anxiety disorders, and 28 percent from social phobia. They also are more likely to have risky health behaviors such as alcohol abuse, which affects 52 percent of men with PTSD and 28 percent of women, while drug abuse is seen in 35 percent of men and 27 percent of women with PTSD.[3]

In 1 out of 10 Americans, the traumatic event causes a cascade of psychological and biological changes known as post-traumatic stress disorder." [4]

[2] Va.gov: Veterans Affairs. How Common is PTSD in Adults? (2018, September 13). Retrieved March 8, 2022, from https://www.ptsd.va.gov/understand/common/common_adults. asp#:~:text=The%20following%20statistics%20are%20based,have%20gone%20through%20 a%20trauma

[3] Va.gov: Veterans Affairs. How Common is PTSD in Adults? (2018, September 13). Retrieved March 8, 2022, from https://www.ptsd.va.gov/understand/common/common_adults.asp

[4] Veteransinfo. (2019, August 13). PTSD. VETERANS INFORMATION. Retrieved March 8, 2022, from http://veteransinfo.org/ptsd.html

According to the National Trauma Institute:[5]

The economic burden of trauma is more than $585 billion every year. People who have experienced trauma are:

- 15 times more likely to attempt suicide
- 4 times more likely to become an alcoholic
- 4 times more likely to develop a sexually transmitted disease
- 4 times more likely to inject drugs
- 3 times more likely to use antidepressant medication
- 3 times more likely to be absent from work
- 3 times more likely to experience depression
- 3 times more likely to have serious job problems
- 2.5 times more likely to smoke
- 2 times more likely to develop chronic obstructive
- pulmonary disease (COPD)
- 2 times more likely to have serious financial problems

Regardless of these grim statistics, it is possible to heal. When traumas are worked with effectively, healing can be fast, profound, and long-lasting.

Benefits of Healing Trauma and the Trauma of Shame Break Free From:

- Limiting beliefs
- Vicious cycles
- Reenactments
- Progress followed by pullback
- Toxic shame
- Negative self-talk
- Social anxiety
- Fear of being seen
- Fear of not being heard
- Lack of confidence

5 Va.gov: Veterans Affairs. How Common is PTSD in Adults? (2018, September 13). Retrieved March 8, 2022, from https://www.ptsd.va.gov/understand/common/common_adults.asp

- Low self-esteem
- Shyness
- Fear of incompetence
- Self-destructive behaviors
- Self-sabotage
- Habits
- Addictions
- Self-harm
- PTSD symptoms
- Panic
- Anxiety
- Generalized fears
- Intrusive thoughts
- Flashbacks
- Reliving
- Depression
- Feeling defeated
- Futility
- Suppressed Anger
- Grief
- Regret
- Dissociation
- Hypervigilance
- Emotional volatility
- Lack of emotionality
- Collapse

Let me tell you about an extraordinary case study.

Many years ago, I was contacted by a client who hadn't left his house in eight years. He wanted to see me in person rather than videoconferencing, but that was intrinsically a challenge. He came up with a plan to have a friend drive him the hour and a half to my home office in Los Angeles. He stood on the front porch with a blanket over his head when I answered the door. Concerned with what the neighbors might think, I quickly ushered him inside. Knowing that this may be the only opportunity I had to see him in person, I worked with him for two hours.

At the end of the session, he said, "I used to come into Hollywood years ago. There's a Chinese restaurant nearby that has a really good duck. I think I'm going to go have the duck."

My greatest wish for you, dear reader, is that you will use this book as a roadmap for your intrapersonal healing and transformation. I firmly believe without hesitation, you will find a renewed sense of hope that healing is possible and that trauma and the trauma of shame are not life sentences.

The healing journey can be an 'awakening' to untapped resources and help you achieve an increased sense of vitality and flow. You will strengthen your sense of connection to yourself and others. Once you restore your nervous system to resilience and disempower old limiting unconscious beliefs, then you can live your best life. It is your birthright to experience life on Planet Earth with curiosity, excitement, and the fulfillment of whatever your needs and desires may be.

PART TWO

MYTH BUSTING
WHAT WON'T WORK AND WHY

You're Not Broken Beyond Repair

*U*ntil now, you just haven't understood what trauma is, how you have been traumatized, the effects of ongoing trauma in your life, or how to effectively heal your trauma. To fully recover, first, you have to understand what's truly wrong. Once you can pinpoint the root cause or original wound, then it is possible to work with it in a way that is most likely going to facilitate real and profound healing.

Some wounds, like a stubbed toe, will heal on their own, even though there are protocols that will ensure a speedier recovery. So it may be, after all, that you are not broken beyond repair but simply may have been unwittingly misplacing your focus and attention.

You may have been victimized in the past, but you don't need to be a victim of your past.

The wounds of trauma are more like broken bones. To heal properly, the bone must be set back into place and given the time it needs to repair. The good news is that the wounds of trauma also heal like bones; a broken bone becomes sound by knitting itself back together even stronger than it was before. Bones also become denser in response to repetitive stress. So that which doesn't kill you actually does make you stronger.

Trauma, when not properly treated, continues to fester. No amount of mental gymnastics can fully renegotiate the original wounding experience nor reorganize the long-lasting impacts of unresolved trauma. Trauma is cyclical, meaning it can go dormant and periodically resurface. When the original wound truly heals, the presenting symptoms you have been struggling with will naturally go away. When symptoms periodically abate but continue to return, it indicates that the underlying cause has still not been addressed.

A diagnosis is a name given for a collection of symptoms when enough people present the same set of baffling symptoms. Most people stop their inquiry with a diagnosis. They fail to seek the cause and, therefore, fail to find the cure. And all too often, when a treatment is formulated, it is provided by Big Pharma.

Fibromyalgia is one such example. People who suffer from those symptoms now have a diagnosis, but until there is an effective pharmaceutical treatment, it will remain under the generalized diagnosis of other 'invisible diseases.' But at least those suffering are no longer being made to feel like they are crazy. For so long, they were told that it was all 'just in their heads.' No, it's not in their heads, Doc; it is real, and it is in their bodies. Thankfully, the one thing Western medicine can agree on now is that fibromyalgia seems to be from an 'overactive' nervous system. I guess that's, in part, why I have had such a success rate in working with fibromyalgia patients—because I work on the original wounds that continue to dysregulate the nervous system.

Another example, decades ago, I had a massage client who complained of a chronic tight lower back and hip. It caused him nearly constant pain and discomfort. Consequently, I would see him once or twice a week. He had had x-rays and an MRI that showed compression in the lumbar spine and a rotated hip. He was satisfied with his diagnosis and put all of his attention, time, and money into managing his pain. He knew he was consuming too many analgesics. And on occasion, his frustration would send him to acupuncturists, chiropractors, and other types of bodyworkers. But he refused to go to physical therapy because of the inconvenience of the twice-a-week crosstown drive and because the prescribed exercises required physical effort on his behalf.

I had spoken with him on several occasions that the source of his pain must have been from his posture or repetitive movement. Then one night after our session, he asked me to join him in his home office because he had forgotten to write a check for me. I discovered the root cause of his pain from the moment I stepped foot into his office. I could see a deep impression in the sofa cushion where he spent most of his days. His hip dropped into the overstuffed down cushion when he sat as he crossed his legs and leaned onto the threadbare arm. The years of pain and discomfort, the countless hours of different therapies, the handfuls of Tylenol he consumed were all in vain and ultimately unnecessary. When he followed my advice and simply repositioned himself and sat at the other end of the sofa, his constant companion of chronic pain dramatically reduced. After a few weeks of physical therapy (including traction), the compression in his lumbar spine was released. His hip was rehabilitated and returned to its proper alignment.

I have told that story as an analogy to help put into perspective the dire need to find the genesis of your strife. You may have spent years trying to change the external environment (the details and circumstances of your life) to change the internal environment (the way you feel). But when we change the internal environment, the external environment has to reflect it.

"If I had that car, house, or watch, I'd feel like a success."

"If I pray, practice yoga, and meditate regularly, I will have internal peace, calm, and serenity."

"If I could just get out of this town, I could finally be my true Self."

"If I were in a relationship, then I would feel safe and happy."

None of these statements are without virtue. In fact, they all may ring true for you. Yet, not one of them is a universal truth. Millionaires and billionaires commit suicide. I prayed, meditated, and practiced yoga regularly, and I could barely string a few blissful hours together.

It is also crucial that you have realistic expectations. All too often, I have clients who come to me to liberate them from any kind of discomfort so they can experience a life of what I call (with lighthearted-tongue-in-cheekiness) 'the rama-lama-ding-dong of eternal bliss.' They earnestly want me to release them from the shackles of anything that separates them from their divine right to attain a hedonistic level of abundance and everlasting exquisite elation and ecstasy—yesterday.

It seems that, as a culture, we are now living in the delusion that our lives should be void of stress and worry, and if we are not in a constant state of calm, relaxation, ease, grace, contentment, and peace, then we think something is wrong. If we are unable, after several attempts, to get into and remain in that state of peace, then there is something wrong with us. In truth, inner turmoil serves us and has purpose. If it were even possible to sustain that kind of peace, it would soon flatline and would no longer feel so warm and fuzzy and ooey and gooey.

Some people would say that they have already experienced all the pain and discomfort, and all that they want and deserve now is to move forward into the monotony of grace.

But we have to have a reference point that clarifies right from wrong, light from dark, holy from evil. In order to experience the middle ground of centeredness, we have to be in that space which is neither left nor right, top nor bottom, and front nor back. We need the emotional lows to be able to relish the sweet nectar of emotional highs. Without pain, there would be no pleasure.

Perhaps real success lies in the intrapersonal awareness that we are proud of who we are and have created a sense of safety for ourselves in the world. It stands to reason that the need for self-soothing behaviors and spiritual practices is precipitated by the internal static and discord that plagues us. It's pretty likely that if we don't go within, then we will go without. And, if we could get out of our own way, we could very well discover and become our best Self.

Without a doubt, talk therapy and psychotropic medications change and save lives. Their merit and value are beyond measure. However, many medications also have well-known side effects, including but not limited to psychosis, suicidal ideation and depersonalization, derealization, and dissociation. As Gendlin's research indicated, the therapist and the type of therapy must complement the client and the issues they seek help for. Not all therapists are perfectly suited for all clients any more than every therapeutic approach is appropriate for any disorder. That said, even the most highly skilled and talented therapist who is a master at creating a safe container for the client and establishing impeccable rapport may not be best suited for working specifically with trauma. Many good therapists will refer their clients to a trauma-informed practitioner in such cases.

There are pioneers in the field like Dr. Peter Levine, who has been teaching mental health practitioners since 1972. His technique, Somatic Experiencing, is considered one of the most effective treatments for healing developmental trauma and shock traumas. Anxiety, panic, and PTSD, as well as most syndromes, are trauma-based, and I find the results of this work are even more far-reaching than that.

And yet, I continually meet traditional talk therapists from various disciplines who have never heard of Dr. Levine, Somatic Experiencing, or any other somatic approach. Those who may not be well informed might be doing a disservice to some of their clients without realizing it.

The Somatic Experiencing International website states, "Somatic Experiencing (SE™) is a body-oriented therapeutic model applied in multiple professions and professional settings—psychotherapy, medicine, coaching, teaching, and physical therapy—for healing trauma and other stress disorders. It is based on a multidisciplinary intersection of physiology, psychology, ethology, biology, neuroscience, indigenous healing practices, and medical biophysics and has been clinically applied for more than four decades.

The SE approach releases traumatic shock, which is key to

transforming PTSD and the wounds of emotional and early developmental attachment trauma. It offers a framework to assess where a person is 'stuck' in the fight, flight or freeze responses and provides clinical tools to resolve these fixated physiological states. SE provides effective skills appropriate to a variety of healing professions including mental health, medicine, physical and occupational therapies, bodywork, addiction treatment, first response, education, and others."[6]

Fortunately, trauma and shame have gained much attention as of late within the mental health industry. At the beginning of my career as a trauma specialist, I spent much of my time educating people about trauma and why it needs to be worked with somatically. Of course, I still do, hence why I wrote this book. But I have noticed, especially in the past five or six years, that more people are specifically searching for trauma-informed therapists or specialized practitioners, like myself, who work exclusively with trauma somatically.

During the Somatic Experiencing trainings that I have assisted over the years, I often witness rooms full of therapists marvel at how old wounds resurface within themselves that they thought they had already resolved. Perhaps part of the reason for this is that talking about past trauma can re-traumatize.

---

[6] SE 101. Somatic Experiencing® International. (2022, February 15). Retrieved March 15, 2022, from https://traumahealing.org/se-101/

Shortcuts

We are inundated with so many offers of salvation filling our email boxes and Facebook feeds that navigating the labyrinth of self-help and supported help can be overwhelming and anxiety-provoking in and of itself. There appear to be more paths for healing than there are issues that need to be healed. We are being sold more snake oil from charlatans than ever before.

And everyone loves the idea of the magic bullet or the magic carpet ride. Many throw mountains of cash at a plethora of quick fixes and secret formulas. Take this pill; repeat this mantra; do this practice; say this prayer (even if in a different language than the one you speak). These shortcuts promise to liberate us from a host of conditions and disorders but rarely do they focus on what creates the vicious cycles of self-defeating patterns, anxiety, panic, hopelessness, despair, resentment, or depression. Time and time again, we are sold a bill of goods that promises to teleport us into a world of moonbeams, unicorns, pixie dust, peace, unbridled success, contentment, and joyfulness. Time and time again, these helpful and well-intended practices don't work because, in general, they do not address the root causes or original wounds.

By no means am I diminishing the undeniable value of many, if not all, spiritual, cognitive, and behavioral practices. I genuinely believe that every path has a following and every seeker finds a path. Some people meditate and pray in an effort to deepen their own awareness and welcome, courageously, the insights and discomfort that call them within. There are true spiritual warriors, who love the physical, metaphysical, and mental journey, as well as the benefits, gleaned from their pursuits. Religion and faith can sustain us even when there is no other resource, physical support, or sense of hope.

Regardless of your back-breaking efforts to exert mind over matter, implementing spiritual practices, and experimenting with medications and behavior modifications, you may have found, like me, that the results were minimal or, at best, short term. Although some of what you are doing may seem to be helping, it might also just be a temporary fix.

When are prayer, meditation, and yoga no different from sex, drugs, and rock 'n' roll? There is very little difference when they are being used as a means to self-regulate. In simplistic terms, we are self-regulating any time we try to change the way we currently feel. We all need a break, at times, from what we are thinking and feeling, but there is an intrinsic difference between doing something to avoid or resist feeling what you are feeling and embracing a practice of devotion. Most add value to our lives. Some, like prayer and meditation, are undeniably beneficial and healing.

Unfortunately, not all ways of self-regulation are always healing mechanisms. The fundamental distinction lies in intention and application. They are excellent choices when seen for what they indeed are, a means for temporary self-soothing. But their limitations are often not seen, and instead, they are seen as a potential panacea.

Cognitive and psychological inquiry can help shift perspective and reframe past pain. We can rationalize and diminish the deeply felt meaning of painful memories and condition ourselves into a new way of thinking. Denial and her first cousin, suppression, help us to push things into the background because we have been told that if we don't acknowledge it, then it doesn't exist. Navigating the labyrinth of self-help and supported help can be overwhelming. And more often than not, we also have the even more dubious task of trying to free ourselves from our own deeply set defense and belief systems. These systems may have served us at one time, but have become maladapted and detrimental over time. These antiquated systems might even be a major part of the formation and sustainability of our current issues and can keep us from being able to truly heal.

Spiritual Bypass

Personally, I wondered, 'Why was it that mantras, The Secret, affirmations, The Law of Attraction, vision boards, and creative visualizations seemed to work for others, but not for me? Why couldn't I find the right seminar, formulate the perfect affirmations, simply visualize the future the way I wanted to live it, or just change my negative thoughts into positive ones? And, why should I have to venture into the trenches of my past, when everyone else seems to have gotten a 'Get out of jail free card'?'

Honestly, in retrospect, they had helped to some degree. They gave me a reprieve, a temporary respite from my internal hell. But, sadly, they also created an incredible sense of false hope and the whiplash of a massive shame spiral. Why did all of these new thought principles and spiritual practices seem to be working for everyone else, while making me even more aware of the chasm that existed between who I was and the person I wanted to be? Why was the place I wanted to be in my life always beyond my reach?

But now, in hindsight, I can be honest with myself. I never meditated, prayed, or took a yoga class for the sake of the long-term benefits on my mental, physical, or spiritual health. Granted, I always felt better afterward. Temporarily.

I had a slew of bypass systems in place to help me manage and maintain (avoid and resist) my persistent negative thoughts and uncomfortable feelings until the next class or book or pill. The melange of collage and decoupage vision boards that I had Elmer-glued proved it. There must be something so incredibly wrong or damaged about me. It wasn't fair! I said my affirmations out loud with emotion every day. I imagined myself careening down the California Pacific Coast Highway in a shiny brand-new Porsche convertible, wearing a gold Rolex with the wind in my hair, feeling elated and grateful for the abundance in my life. I watched the mind-movie that I created religiously. I prayed and meditated. I licked the toad, drank the jungle goo, and altered my consciousness by every means possible.

And I was still here. Still struggling. Still me.

I never had time to read fiction; instead, I read, highlighted, and dog-eared most of the pages of Abraham Hicks' Law of Attraction books, several books of the late great Wayne Dyer, Shakti Gawain's *Creative Visualization*, and Neale Donald Walsch's *Conversations with God*. I bathed in their words and trusted that completing all of the recommended exercises would deliver me into a blissful way of living.

Little did I know at the time that I was trying to leverage spiritual and exoteric pursuits to avoid or resist the ways I was feeling. I never stopped to think that perhaps my attention and efforts would be more impactful if I first took the time to heal the wounds that caused the problems that I was trying to fix. I, like many others, tried to drown out my reality by surrendering in faith to any and every power greater than me. I had no qualms if the transformation I sought came from the Holy Bible, Torah, Quran, Bhagavad Gita, or a Native American medicine man. I sought salvation by any and every means.

I learned and grew and gleaned much, but I didn't find the profound healing that I had hoped for. Apparently, as I later came to discover, I was rudderless and at sea in a deluge of spiritual bypass.

A spiritual bypass or spiritual bypassing "is to sidestep or avoid facing unresolved emotional issues, psychological wounds, and unfinished developmental tasks. The term was introduced in the early 1980s by John Welwood, a Buddhist teacher and psychotherapist."[7]

Robert Augustus Masters, details the telltale signs of this defense system in his book, *Spiritual Bypassing: When Spirituality Disconnects Us From What Really Matters.*

He says, "Whenever I became anxious, I would immediately reach for the nearest Eckhart Tolle or Alan Watts text on my bookshelf. Instead of sitting with the anxiety and checking in to see if it was coming from an innocuous source, I would quickly find refuge in spiritual philosophy. [And] I would strive to maintain the appearance of someone who is constantly at peace with oneself, even though inside I may have felt like the weight of the world was crushing down on my soul. This kind of faux spirituality had a complete stranglehold on my speech and behavior and caused intense cognitive dissonance."[8]

[7] Wikimedia Foundation. (2021, October 15). Spiritual bypass. Wikipedia. Retrieved March 8, 2022, from https://en.wikipedia.org/wiki/Spiritual_bypass
[8] Masters, R. A. (2010). Spiritual bypassing: When spirituality disconnects us from what really matters. North Atlantic Books.

The following passage is from Jeff Brown, the founder of the Soulshaping Institute and author of *Soulshaping, Love it Forward, An Uncommon Bond*, and *Ascending with Both Feet on the Ground*.

"The spiritual bypass is the tendency to jump to spirit prematurely, usually in an effort to avoid various aspects of earthly reality (practical challenges, unresolved emotions and memories). The bypass has many symptoms—the starry-eyed bliss trip, radical detachment from one's self-identifications, premature forgiveness, ungrounded behaviors, wish-full thinking, etc."[9]

Professionally, spiritual bypass is perhaps the trickiest of the bypass systems to circumvent. Religious beliefs and spiritual platitudes are steeped in unsurpassed morality while hidden in the cloaks of superiority that can't be questioned by their very nature. Unshakeable faith is lauded beyond measure and requires no justification.

I was skating on thin ice whenever I broached the subject of spiritual bypass with clients. I faced the same potential reaction and consequence as when a grandparent calls into question the child-rearing choices of their progeny.

One day, I found this out the hard way. Even though I proposed the concept cautiously through self-disclosure of my own personal experience, the oxygen was quickly sucked out of the room. I could tell my client couldn't wait to escape the formerly safe environs of my office to 'Om Shanti' himself

[9] Rumford, D. J. (1996). Soulshaping. Tyndale House Publishers.

back behind the thin veil of transcendence. It was the last time I was to see him.

Cognitive Bypass

It stands to reason that if you continue to carry out the same thoughts, words, and actions that got you to where you are now, your future will undoubtedly look just like your past. Most people would like to think that the past is over and done and, now, all that they need to concern themselves with is to imagine a better future and align their thoughts, words, and actions with those fantastical images. Indeed our thoughts, words, and actions are integral to manifesting our future, but simply strong-arming your thoughts, policing your words, and strong-arming your actions can't even begin to compete with your old limiting beliefs.

It was 1984, and I had just finished reading Shirley MacLaine's *Out on a Limb*. Although it had been chalked up to the way-out ramblings of just another Hollywood wackadoodle, Ms. MacLaine's book cracked open the coconut of my limited, granular thinking. Then Louise Hay's book *You Can Heal Your Life* shoved a stick of dynamite into the fissure and shattered my former sense of reality beyond recognition.

I consumed and absorbed *You Can Heal Your Life*, which, to date, has sold over 35 million copies in 30 languages. I couldn't put the book down. I read it on the New York City subway to and from work, on my break during my shift waiting tables, while shoveling food into my face, and every other waking moment.

I repeated the affirmations by rote, excited in anticipation of the ideas manifesting themselves into my reality. But alas, the weeks and months that passed bore no real tangible results. Regardless, I kept the faith, and I kept rereading her book.

Louise Hay's book was literally the beginning of the New Age movement. At the time, there wasn't a self-help section in any bookstore. But the New Age books marked a turning point in my life and so many others'. I knew I had stumbled onto something epic and beyond my current comprehension, and I longed for the holy grail that they extolled as possible. It's not that mystics and seekers hadn't existed for eons, but these books marked the beginning of the matriculation of New Thought into mainstream American culture.

Reading those two books forever changed the course of my life. There was simply no way to find my way back; there was no trail of breadcrumbs. I found myself in an uncharted forest without a compass. I felt so desperately alone; however, the only way to re-establish a sense of connection to others in this new world would be to bring them with me, if they were ready, willing, and able. I ran to the closest bookstore, purchased all 33 remaining copies of Ms. Hay's primer to intrapersonal transformation books and the remaining 16 copies of Ms. MacLaine's epic journey into the great beyond, and gave them away to friends and strangers, hoping to build a tribe of seekers beyond the norm.

I can't recall how I came across Shakti Gawain's book, *Creative Visualization*. But I believe I saw a poster at my favorite crystal store in Manhattan for her upcoming workshop. (Yes, I even got into the crystal craze.) I wondered if my results with repeating affirmations were limited because I needed to visualize them. So I ponied up the course fee and one day found myself sitting at the feet of Shakti, herself. I discovered that day that my imagining skills weren't up to snuff. I tried to follow along with her guided meditation of seeing all of my dreams in pink bubbles floating closer and closer to me. Although I practiced daily, there were no offers of a starring role on Broadway or even a lead in a commercial, and, frustratingly, no buckets full of cash appeared. In fact, the more I affirmed my needs and desires and the manifestation of my dreams, the further away they all seemed.

But my pursuit was relentless. I continued to consume the works of Florence Scovel Shinn, Don Miguel Ruiz, Paulo Coelho, and Tony Robbins. I became convinced that knowledge is power, and if I could change my thoughts, I could change my life.

When negative thoughts appeared, like a friend of mine had taught me, I would say, "Cancel/Clear!" and replace it with a positive thought.

I would tell myself things like:
That which doesn't kill me makes me stronger.
It's like water off a duck's back.
If it's going to be, it's up to me.
I've got this; I don't need help.

Thank you, thank you, thank you. I am so truly blessed and grateful. Thank you for the myriad of miracles that I now receive in gratitude.

In time, however, I discovered that knowledge isn't power after all; it's crazy-making until it's applied. Otherwise, it is just like having a head full of AA and a belly full of booze. Denial and rationalization are the lifeblood of cognitive bypass.

No matter how fervently I tried, I couldn't rationalize it all away, telling myself, *The past is the past, and I am going to forge a new path and never look back.* I had become lost in the delusion that I could simply take the multitude of wounding experiences of my past and package them up into a strong box with a beautiful bow and shove them onto a shelf, deep within the recesses of my mind, never to be seen or heard from again.

Behavioral Bypass

The living room window of my last NYC apartment had perfectly framed the iconic Twin Towers. September 11, 2001, forever changed many things, including my relationship to food.

Watching the World Trade Center crumble felt like I was watching a movie, but the reality of what was unfolding live on my TV in Los Angeles was terrifying. I imagined that if it was happening in NYC, LA would be next.

So I did what any sane, rational person would do: I immediately threw all of my dietary restrictions out the window, marched into the kitchen, and made myself a peanut butter and jelly, potato chip, and banana sandwich. Frankly, I was shocked that I even had the ingredients of my all-time favorite childhood sandwich. Granted, it wasn't Jif peanut butter and Lay's potato chips on Wonder bread, but raw, organic almond butter and thick, waffle-cut, organic sea-salt potato chips on a sprouted nine-grain, wheat-free bread. I then went to the bank, pulled out all of my money, and shoved it under my mattress. And for the weeks to come, while conducting internet searches of the safest places on Earth to live, I proceeded to self-soothe my way through my entire childhood menu of Southern comfort foods, one smothered sausage-gravy biscuit and Crisco fried chicken leg at a time.

The world was about to end, so what difference was it going to make if I were vegan, vegetarian, pescatarian, raw, or Paleo? (Now I'll eat anything that's not red-hot or nailed down.)

Many people practice yoga for the sheer joy of it, to release painful chronic holding patterns, or to deepen into a spiritual practice. Others meditate because of its countless benefits, regardless of their current successes or struggles. Across the world, throngs of devotees pray to feel a conscious contact with a higher power, not just to pray away their problems or to avoid accountability by 'handing it over to God.'

It seems that I had it all wrong for many years. If I were frustrated, I would meditate (or medicate). If I felt lack, I would fervently pray for what I wanted. If I were unhappy, I consciously envisioned a radically different future. I understand now that, like me, many people adopt highly orchestrated distracting behaviors to avoid feeling what they are feeling.

I used to practice yoga six days a week, not because I enjoyed the social aspect of class or because I wanted to get into shape. I didn't feel particularly comfortable chanting in Sanskrit, nor did I believe that by doing so, the sound and vibration of the words would resonate in my body and burn karma, all the while elevating my prana or life force. Most of the time, I wasn't even in the room. I completely dissociated and left my body. I just needed a place where I could check out and stop the near-constant negative chatter and cyclical thinking. More often than not, it seemed to work. At least I had a few hours a day when my mind wasn't eating me alive.

I was simply willing to suffer through the drive across town and the high cost of class because I felt different afterward. The problem was that the high I felt while driving home only lasted for a few hours. The next day, I needed to go to class again to change the way I was feeling.

Behavioral bypass is also known as self-regulation or self-soothing. More often than not, this is one of the more unconscious forms of bypass. For many, behavioral bypass has morphed into a way of life.

If I am angry, I go for a run. If I feel lost and hopeless, I go to church. If I'm stressed out, I take a hot bath.

We develop highly skilled methods of distraction, which seem to be the number-one go-to in our arsenal of avoidance techniques. They help, but they can also become an endless loop of chasing our own tails. In fact, our habituated unconscious behaviors can be the very things that keep us from being able to heal. By staying busy and distracted, we're able to avoid dealing with that which needs to be dealt with the most.

As Gabby Bernstein says in her book *Happy Days*, "In the early days of my sobriety, I didn't have the tools for healing the root cause of my addiction. In fact, I didn't even know a deeper wound existed. So while I put down the drink and the drugs, I was still acting out in addictive ways in efforts to control the unconscious impermissible feelings that I couldn't possibly face. I became a work addict. And I was praised for it! People would say things like, 'Wow, Gabby, you get so much done!' or 'You're so impressive!' It was not only socially acceptable to be a work addict, but it was something people admired. All the while, I was avoiding true healing because it was too terrifying to face my unconscious pain."[10]

Being still and quiet can feel vulnerable and dangerous because that is when our thoughts can take over, and feelings begin to surface. We find so many ways to redirect our attention away from what truly matters. Busy work, household chores, watching TV, reading, social media, and the black hole of internet searches can sweep us into other worlds, far away from our own.

[10] Bernstein, G. (2022). Happy days: The guided path from trauma to profound freedom and inner peace. Hay House, Inc.

Sometimes self-soothing or self-regulating behaviors become a problem in and of themselves. Coming home after a hard day at work and having a cocktail to distance yourself from daily stressors is an innocuous ritual. However, over time, it could develop into a drinking problem. It may have started out as a fairly common marker of the end of the workday, but it has the potential to progress to the point where you are hiding a pint of vodka in the back of the toilet. That which at one time helped to soothe and relax you has now become a problem.

As I've mentioned before, one of my survival strategies was to dissociate. (Dissociation is an instinctual response and an incredibly effective survival strategy when we are able to move in and out of it. It's entirely a different story when we get stuck in it, like in depersonalization.) It was a way for me to protect myself. It's not that it was a conscious decision or choice. I didn't even know what I was doing. It was a reflex at best. Over time, it became so ingrained in me that it became a way of life; I lost my sense of direction and the ability to connect to other people.

I remember as a child, when my parents took me to the movies, and the audience would laugh, I would think to myself, Remember that! That is what people think is funny. If they would shriek in terror, I'd tell myself, Okay! That's what people think is scary.

Daydreaming was also a way for me to get lost in the inner world of my imagination and to check out from the outer world that I found to be overwhelmingly uncomfortable and scary.

The real world would disappear as I got lost in my thoughts and numbed out my worries and troubles. But daydreaming while already being dissociated left me in the ether, connected to the civilization of planet Earth only by a tether as thin as spun silk.

PART THREE

BUILDING THE FOUNDATION
FOR HEALING

A Return to Basics

By now, you may see how the bouts of depression, fits of rage, vicious cycles, relentless patterns in your relationships, behavioral habituations, and reenactments that you struggle with today often relate back to the original wounds of unresolved past traumatic events. Even if you know this to be true deep in your gut—or even if I have managed to convince you through the pages you have read so far—you may still feel like you are at your wits' end.

You may be as frustrated now as I had been for so many

years. After all, how many times have you suffered through flashbacks or talked about the details of your childhood with therapists until you were blue in the face? How long have you mulled over the righteous anger that you feel toward family members, old friends, ex-lovers, and even the behaviors of strangers or politicians? How many hours have you spent crying about it alone in the corner of your closet, hoping that the yards of fabric would muffle the sounds of your despair?

Regardless of how skilled you may have become in avoidance practices like distraction and denial or in the mental gymnastics of changing the way you think about things, none of them seem to work anymore. Perhaps, as I did, you have reached your threshold and are no longer able to continue to justify spending thousands of dollars on countless workshops and various approaches to healing.

Sometimes, we have to clear our RAM and reboot even on our healing journey. We may have to clear off all the clutter from our proverbial desktop. With a clean and empty surface, we then return only the tools and resources we specifically need to get the job done. It doesn't have to feel like starting all over from scratch; it can be a fresh start that begins with a return to basics.

My writing process is a great analogy. When I decided to write this book, it took weeks to find, transpose, and compile all of my dribblings and scribblings in various documents, journals, and software applications. I spent several months poring over the disorganized mess that held the potential of becoming the very book that you are reading now.

Periodically, I would open the files, not knowing where to begin. It was all too much to get my head around. Hundreds of thousands of black characters on an incalculable number of white pages, of which I could only see a few paragraphs at a time. I read and organized and reread and reorganized. Cut, copy, and paste. Drag and drop. The nebulous slowly began to take shape but remained out of focus.

Then one day, when I was busy in the middle of doing nothing, an errant memory popped into my mind of me sitting at my little desk in grade school as Ms. Nolde dragged her chalk across the blackboard, her fingers white with dust. She drilled and grilled us on diagramming sentences, a mind-numbing endeavor that I was convinced at the time was baseless, as I could never imagine in my seven-year-old brain when I was ever going to use this in 'real life.' The image cross-faded into me sitting at a larger desk in Mr. Green's advanced English class. He held the chalk in his spotlessly clean fingers, protected by a red rubber chalk condom, which paradoxically failed to keep the white dust from speckling the front of his shirt, which then matched the dandruff drift on his shoulders. The task at hand was creating an outline for a short story that we were supposed to have already read. Even if I had read it, the assignment seemed bass-ackward to me at the time. And the idea of taking the extra time to write an outline seemed like an unnecessary step. Wouldn't that take the creative part out of creative writing?

And just like that, it fell onto me like a ton of bricks—perhaps a return to rudimentary nuts and bolts was in order.

Eureka!

Maybe Ms. Nolde and Mr. Green were smarter than they looked. Perhaps I needed to lay the foundation and build the structure before picking out the paint colors and sending out invitations for the housewarming.

I needed to write an outline for my book. Perhaps then I could bring order to the melee.

Sometimes, it is hard to gain clarity around what you have done on your healing journey that has been effective when you have tried so many different things over an extended period of time. And all that you have done may ultimately serve you better with a strong foundation in place. With the foundation in place, you can then assemble the scaffolding with all of the ancillary skills and tools that you have collected along the way. Then you can unpack the boxes, hang the drapes, arrange the furniture, and make your house your safe home.

Much of this book's focus is to elucidate what trauma is. My aim is to distinguish it from the numerous disorders that one would traditionally seek out the support of a talk therapist for and therefore showcase how to treat trauma differently and more effectively. But no matter how you slice it or dice it, you will still have to roll up your sleeves, put on your game face, and lean in to feel your way through the discomfort and vulnerability in the right way.

You will need to start with the basics, no matter how tedious that might seem. Doing so made writing this book possible, just like it will make healing your trauma possible.

The leading research can be confusing and contradictory, not only because it focuses predominantly on post-traumatic stress disorder but because trauma is much more nuanced than that. Working specifically with developmental and shock traumas requires a different and more highly specialized approach than talk therapy. Attempting to treat trauma with the traditional top-down model of the narrative leading toward catharsis or problem-seeking and problem-solving may not only be counterintuitive but contraindicated.

" . . . that was a problem in the therapies at that time which were very cathartic—really big reactions. And often people would feel better after that—probably, at least in large part, because there was a releasing of endorphins and catecholamines, adrenaline-like hormones, and neurotransmitters, and so the people, in a way, they felt a tremendous relief, even a high. But then they would go back into the same trauma patterns afterwards."
- Dr. Peter A. Levine

The good news is that there are more effective bottom-up techniques available now. Finding the perfect combination of technique, practitioner, and setting (in-person vs. telehealth) can be traumatizing in and of itself, which can affirm the commonplace sense among trauma survivors of futility and the shameful feeling of being broken and unfixable. Every human being is a fingerprint, and so is their trauma history; therefore, there is no cookie-cutter approach.

There are some things you can do alone, and some things are best served with the support and guidance of a trained professional who has developed and mastered the necessary skills. Finding the right kind of specialist is integral. You wouldn't want to go to an aesthetician to treat an unrelenting case of gastric distress any more than you would to go to a dog groomer to get your hair cut.

Unequivocally, the greatest opportunities for intrapersonal healing and growth exist within hardships. Without hesitation, I can declare that the most difficult times of my life propelled me into new paradigms like a quantum leap—but only when I met the challenges I was facing with curiosity and grit. Regardless, there were still occasions when I felt as though I were whirling blindly in the midst of the chaos and bedlam, trying as I might to hold on to that truth like a pitbull's jaws locked down on a tennis ball. There were many times that I doubted I would rise from the ashes.

First things first.

One step at a time.

Trauma

I have certainly been concerned that the tagline for my book, *What to do when self-help or talk therapy hasn't really helped*, might ruffle the feathers of some of my peers, colleagues, and students. Again, by no means am I discounting or diminishing the importance and efficacy of either self-help or supported help. About 40 percent of my private practice are mental health professionals. The vast majority of the more than 120,000 Somatic Experiencing practitioners, who work in 30 countries on 6 continents, are licensed, mental health providers. I also teach mental health professionals how to effectively work with healthy shame and how to heal toxic shame. I am simply saying that truly healing trauma and the trauma of shame requires an additional and more specific set of skills.

It has been a long, hard road for somatic approaches for healing trauma to be recognized and embraced within the field of psychology. Thankfully, that zeitgeist has occurred. However, there is still a long way to go.

According to the American Psychological Association's website, "Trauma is an emotional response to a terrible event like an accident, rape or natural disaster. Immediately after the event, shock and denial are typical. Longer-term reactions include unpredictable emotions, flashbacks, strained relationships and even physical symptoms like headaches or nausea. While these feelings are normal, some people have difficulty moving on with their lives. Psychologists can help these individuals find constructive ways of managing their emotions."[11]

"APA is the leading scientific and professional organization representing psychology in the United States, with more than 133,000 researchers, educators, clinicians, consultants and students as its members."[12]

So, the leading organization of psychologists believes that 'trauma is an emotional response' that can have 'longer term reactions' and even has 'physical symptoms like headaches or nausea.' And psychologists can help those struggling with the

11 American Psychological Association. (n.d.). Trauma and shock. American Psychological Association. Retrieved March 8, 2022, from https://www.apa.org/topics/trauma
12 American Psychological Association. (n.d.). About Apa. American Psychological Association. Retrieved March 8, 2022, from https://www.apa.org/about

aftermath of trauma 'find constructive ways of managing their emotions.' Limiting the physical symptoms to headaches and nausea is quite the understatement taking into consideration the overabundance of physical symptoms attributed to PTSD, anxiety, depression, depersonalization, and panic attacks.

By that definition, their stance is clear. Trauma is an emotional response with longer-term reactions that can be managed. Therefore, since trauma is not that, the approach of traditional psychology is not focused on actually healing trauma but on helping to manage the symptoms of trauma.

This is most likely why so many clients, including mental health professionals, have told me that working with a traditional talk therapist had not helped them resolve their past traumas. In fact, many said that they think that it made things worse for them.

Retelling our stories can re-traumatize—repetitively pick the scabs off those old wounds.

Finding 'constructive ways to manage emotions' is helpful, but it does not address, and rarely is enough to fully resolve the root causes.

Let's now change our focus and look at trauma through the correct lens.

Dr. Peter Levine and many others in the field—like Bessel van der Kolk (author of *The Body Keeps the Score*)—have proven that trauma occurs in the body, not in the event itself or solely in the mind. Trauma is a physiological dysregulation within the brain and nervous system that eventually manifests physical symptoms, emotional responses, limiting beliefs, and repetitive behaviors. When the physiological wounds of trauma are revisited and renegotiated effectively, the presenting symptoms and responses are consequently resolved and will no longer present.

We often think of trauma only in the context of shock traumas, or 'capital T' Traumas like war, accidents, assault, or loss. However, the 'little t' traumas, as in developmental trauma, like emotional abuse, neglect, and shame, are more nefarious and can create even more complicated and lifelong problems. Regardless of whether trauma occurs due to a single event or as a result of chronic, cumulative stress, the body's reactions and long-term changes in perceptions or behaviors remain fairly consistent. Trauma survivors are frequently:

- Angry or emotional
- Dissociative or hypervigilant
- Fearful—feel unsafe in their bodies or the world
- Adrenaline junkies
- Volatile or shut down
- Disconnected or clingy and needy
- Socially anxious or promiscuous
- Untrusting of others, or themselves (insecure)
- Disengaged from life and others
- Self-abusive or violent toward others
- Exhausted/void of life force or unable to sit still
- Dead behind the eyes or wild/wide-eyed
- Prone to panic attacks or collapse
- Disempowered or overpowered

Symptoms of Trauma:

- Self-regulation through sex, drugs, alcohol, exercise, prayer, meditation, food, TV, etc.
- Avoiding memories
- Keeping busy
- Avoiding situations that remind you of the trauma
- Repressing memories (being unable to remember aspects of the event)
- Feeling detached, cut off, and emotionally numb
- Being unable to express affection
- Feeling there's no point in planning for the future
- Being easily upset or angry
- Disturbed sleep
- Irritability and aggressive behavior
- Lack of concentration
- Reliving aspects of the trauma
- Hopelessness
- Extreme alertness
- Panic
- Anxiety
- Being easily startled
- Reliving aspects of the trauma
- Vivid flashbacks (feeling that the trauma is happening all over again)
- Intrusive thoughts and images
- Nightmares
- Intense distress at real or symbolic reminders of the trauma

Trauma-Based Syndromes:

- Fibromyalgia
- Crohn's disease
- Lupus
- Irritable bowel
- Epstein-Barr
- Chronic fatigue
- Colitis
- Tourette's
- Chronic pain
- Restless leg

Wherein lies the dividing line between a stressful event and a traumatic one, and what is it that quantifies and qualifies an event as stressful as opposed to traumatic? Our bodies have innate, non-cognitive defense responses to threats. In simple terms, our defense responses (commonly referred to as freeze, flight, and fight) are engaged when facing threats of any kind, perceived or real. In other words, our primitive or reptilian brains perceive a threat and activate the nervous system into the arousal of survival strategies. That life-force energy mobilizes the body into different sets of behaviors. Some events may be best met with being still and quiet to see if the threat will pass on its own; if the danger persists, then the organism attempts to move away or, as a last resort, to fight.

A threat is anything that portends the possibility of danger or damage. The body reacts to threats the same way regardless of the source of the threat. The same part of the brain lights up when we are facing down a wild animal, the prospect of public speaking, or a social faux pas. Perceptually, failing socially actually has the potential to harm us or hurt us more deeply and profoundly than being attacked by a wild animal. Betrayal, public humiliation, abandonment, and neglect are far more complicated to heal than puncture wounds, abrasions, and lacerations.

Our bodies react to threats regardless if we are cognitively aware that there is a possibility of trouble—like in the first few moments of my car wreck when my higher brain couldn't make any sense of what was going on. I was in mortal danger, and it was my lower brain that took command over the situation. It was all happening too fast for me to think my way through it.

I was facing the very real threat of both physical and energetic boundary rupture. My physical body would likely be crushed or torn apart, and the energetic life force that had animated my body for all of these years would launch into the ether, leaving my body and all that I had known behind. Since I walked away from the wreck relatively unscathed, the threat was perceived, but my body behaved as if it were real. Granted, flipping and rolling a car is definitely a threat, but in reality, my physical injuries were akin to skinning my knee.

The reality of threat isn't just in regard to life-and-death importance. You can experience a sense of energetic boundary rupture of peace and quiet when the next-door neighbor's gardener revs up the leaf blower when you are meditating or enjoying an afternoon siesta. When your partner contemplates leaving you, your vision of the future is at stake. If you have an unexpected major expense, you may fear not being able to pay your mortgage, thereby losing the safety and security of having a roof over your head. Any of these things can cause a stress response.

Following the resolution of the threat, by whatever means, if the nervous system is able to move from the former state of hyperarousal and is then able to naturally unwind and fully discharge the survival energy, then that event is considered to have been stressful. If that process is truncated in any way and the nervous system does not reorganize and return to resilience, then that event is considered to have been traumatic.

So, trauma is a result of incomplete defense responses. When these survival strategies are unable to complete, the system can get stuck in an endless loop, trying to complete the truncated defense responses. That stuck energy in the nervous system creates disorganization and dysregulation: trauma.

Many external stimuli can impact the discharge and reorganization process after the initial threat passes. For instance, we are taught and socialized not to feel ('big boys don't cry' or 'anger is bad'), so the higher brain interprets feeling anything as something being wrong. The brain then sets out to manage or fix the problem or to distract you from feeling it.

Or the higher brain may override the nervous system's ability to self-regulate. If our hands shake or tremble, we might try to stop them by sitting on them or holding them tight. If our breath is short and shallow, we may consciously take long, deep breaths to ease our sense of alarm. By not allowing the body to do what it knows it needs to do to discharge the arousal, we may very well end up traumatizing ourselves.

Without you having to give it a single thought, your nervous system should remain in a constant state of fluctuation, moving between arousal, discharge, and reorganization, and thus, return to homeostasis. We feel in our bodies the nervous system as it escalates into hypervigilance, as well as when it is discharging the arousal. Because we have the ability to modify or change our behavior, emotions, and thoughts, we can get in the way and disrupt the natural cycles of arousal, discharge, and reorganization. We can encourage it or interfere with it.

Some people get stuck in freeze, others get stuck in a flight response, and others stay in an ever-present flight response. We need to have all our instinctual drives online and accessible. Your nervous system wants to discharge, reorganize, and return to homeostasis. So it may be prudent to figure out why it's in the holding pattern in the first place—and then use proven methods to encourage it to unwind and release.

A fascinating study was done where white lab mice's vital signs were monitored while being exposed to the scent of cherry blossoms and simultaneously receiving an electric shock. Obviously, eventually, the mice would have the same reaction to being shocked without the stimulus whenever they smelled cherry blossoms. Not anything groundbreaking, being quite similar to Pavlov's dogs, but what is surprising is that the mice were bred, and for five more generations, they continued to react to the scent of cherry blossoms as if they had been shocked.

So here, we can see that trauma can be transgenerational. An epigenetic marker is passed down from generation to generation to ensure the survival of the offspring in response to a unique environmental threat that, over time, became consistent. Again, this clarifies that trauma is a physiological condition and not wholly a psychological disorder and proves that trauma is so much more than just an emotional issue that can be resolved through talking.

David Sweatt, a neurobiologist at the University of Alabama at Birmingham, who was not involved in the work, calls it "the most rigorous and convincing set of studies published to date demonstrating acquired transgenerational epigenetic effects in a laboratory model."[13]

Both stress and trauma are born in the body's reaction to threat. However, any two humans carrying out the exact same activity in the same location at the same time can have two completely different experiences. How can one person interpret a particular experience as threatening—even traumatizing—while another experiences it as thrilling?

Stress is directly proportional to the degree to which we are not accepting our current circumstances. We can feel stress in our body's response to a situation that we find ourselves in and in reaction to our current thoughts, past memories, and what we imagine about the future. We can feel stress from experiences that pose no threat of physical harm. Stressors can be real, perceived, and even unconscious, yet we feel the same array of physiological reactions.

You can observe this when a bird looks for the early morning worm. As it is pecking the ground, it is simultaneously constantly searching for threats to make sure that the worm is the only breakfast being served that morning. If it detects a possible threat—like the sound of leaves crunching or unusual movement in the nearby brush—then there is no choice but immediate flight. It is purely the mechanism of an instinctual stimulus and response. Even if it could think, it wouldn't take

13 American Psychological Association. (n.d.). About Apa. American Psychological Association. Retrieved March 8, 2022, from https://www.apa.org/about

the time to do so.

On the other hand, humans can fall prey to internal conflict when one part of the brain is in conflict with another. The higher brain cognition can override the lower brain survival instinct. An example of this would be if you were waiting for an elevator at night in a strange building and the doors were to open, and you discovered a strange man already in the lift. You might have a weird feeling in your gut telling you to wait for the next car, but you step in regardless because you don't want to offend him. This is an internal conflict between your Early Detection Warning System (lower brain), your Social Engagement System (middle brain), and your Rational Mind (higher brain). It's like having one foot on the gas and one foot on the brake, which is how many of you may feel like you are living your life.

I look at the lower brain as my guardian angel. Its primary purpose and function is to ensure the survival of the organism. It needs to know 24/7 where you are in time and space. Its constant query is, "Am I safe?" It establishes whether or not you are safe from the information it collects from the higher brain, the middle brain, and through the five senses.

The first and best defense response for either predator or prey when facing a threat of any kind, perceived or real, is to freeze. Freezing provides a few best-case scenario. When immobilized in fear, the physiology of the body contracts to become as small and still as possible to avoid detection. If the potential outside threat escalates, then the system can literally shut itself down—or feign death—to disengage from the predator/ prey response. The predator needs the prey response. If the prey is nonresponsive, the predator may lose interest.

Hiding or collapsing conserves energy, reduces risk, and increases the likelihood of survival. The freeze response also provides time for assessment, like what happened during my automobile accident when time slowed down. Is the danger real? Will the threat pass on its own? Is hiding a viable option? Biologically, do sugars and fats in the system need to be quickly accessed to provide extra energy to the musculature?

The next best choice to avoid imminent peril is to flee. Our legs serve a dual purpose in the activation of survival strategy. First and foremost, we can utilize the power of our largest and strongest muscles to propel us through space. We can run from harm and toward safety. Although the risk increases and energy is expelled, there is a better chance of survival in escape than fighting with an unknown force.

There is only one option left when all else fails: fighting, which relies on a hierarchy of choices. As with all strategic processes, there is a risk assessment of return on investment. Sometimes, we can leverage our intellectual hypervigilance to avoid a situation before it becomes problematic, or we may call upon the use of sound and words to disempower our foes. Screaming at the top of our lungs can elicit a flight response in the assailant, who then fears being outnumbered if others come to our rescue. Or we may be able to negotiate de-escalation through reasoning or demoralizing the opponent.

When logic and words fail us, we must physically fight to protect ourselves. The further we can keep the threat away from our vital organs, the better, but if the threat persists and the use of our arms and legs don't suffice, then our final line of defense lies in the power of our jaws and the density of our teeth. It's no wonder a human bite can exert 150 to 200 PSI (pounds per square inch)—we only need 70 PSI to eat.

Who can forget when Mike Tyson bit a chunk of Evander Holyfield's ear off? Tyson couldn't use his legs except to evade, his hands and arms were failing him, so instinct kicked in, and he resorted to using his last line of defense.

Developmental Trauma

*O*ur early wounding traumatic experiences can have the most long-lasting impact on us. We are biologically hard-wired to survive, and we need to learn from our mistakes and avoid known threats.

This is also the fundamental structure at work in all of our adult relationships, especially our most intimate ones. In adult intimate relationships, we have a tendency to seek out solutions to our unmet needs and desires from earlier in life. This is also where most conflicts in relationships occur. We all need to feel seen, heard, gotten, acknowledged, and appreciated, and we all have needs and desires that we deserve to have met. The lengths we are willing to go to satisfy these needs prove that our earliest wounds remain the soft underbelly of our current struggles.

An infant has needs and desires. The infant signals by crying, screaming, or cooing when one arises. When that doesn't work, they resort to physical protests, like striking, kicking, biting, or arching their back and pressing their head into the bed. The caregiver's responsive presence and touch can assure the child that they have been heard. A lack of attendance to the child is neglect. Albeit, several generations of parents were taught that it was best to let the child 'cry it out' to avoid a spoiled or overly dependent child. However, consciously withholding or deliberately hurting the child in response to their signals is abuse.

Consequently, infancy is also when we learn many of our defense systems, survival strategies, and coping mechanisms. Unless we work with them effectively, these beliefs and defenses can stay firmly rooted in place for the rest of our lives. As we age and our circumstances change, so should our personalities and rules of engagement, but that is not always the case. In fact, most adults are actually acting like their toddler selves regardless of their current chronological age.

Attunement is effectively assessing and providing the child's need for comfort, care, or pleasure. The more often a child's signals are responded to, the stronger their sense of safety, knowing that they are not alone. Consistently meeting the child's needs and desires instills self-awareness, confidence, self-reliance, and trust in others and the world as a whole. However, when their distress signals or their needs and desires are not attended to, their survival mechanism kicks in, and they fear that they may die. Their cries for help escalate as the desperation for care intensifies. This is such an overwhelming experience, their banks of toleration are breached, and the system eventually collapses into resignation and futility. And the potential of attracting predators outweighs their need for attention.

The impact of early-life trauma such as this reaches far beyond just mental health. If the very people who were supposed to provide care and affection were unable to do so, the presumption is that that will also be the case outside of the home. It can lead to social disengagement, as well as limited cognitive acuity and behavioral problems.

Developmental trauma occurs when a child's distress signals are not attuned to and, consequently, their needs and desires are not met well enough, consistently enough, over time. This can teach the child that they have no value or don't matter, or that the world and other people are unsafe or dangerous.

As a defense response, they may become distrusting of others and grow up believing that their needs and desires don't matter or won't be met anyway. To protect themselves from feeling that same pain again, they may keep others at arm's length. They have learned that they can't depend on others, and the greatest chance for survival is to develop strong self-will and become autonomous, regardless of their deep internal drive to find someone who will be able to attune to them and meet their needs and desires.

Or they might come to believe that to connect and belong, the most basic human need, they need to meet the needs and desires of others through people-pleasing, proving that they have value and worth. It may also be difficult for them to recognize their own needs and desires and express what they are, afraid that they would be seen as needy and, therefore, undesirable.

When the primary caretakers are also the source of fear and pain, like growing up in a household where there is danger, violence, neglect, alcoholism, or drug abuse, there is often a conflation of love and affection with fear and pain. In intimate adult relationships, they may find that it doesn't feel like love and affection if there isn't also fear and pain. As counterintuitive as it may seem, they can exhibit behaviors that antagonize their partner or instigate conflict. They also tend to be in a constant state of hypervigilance, finding it challenging to sit still or feel safe. They learned at a very early age how to detect danger in hopes of avoiding it, often catastrophizing the future. They became masters of anticipating the possibility of anything going wrong so that they could have several contingency plans in place if need be.

The beliefs that we form about ourselves, others, and the world at large during the developmental stage of our lives continue to influence us—unless we take the time to revisit the early wounds and resolve them.

Factors that can lead to developmental trauma include:

- Shame
- Abuse
- Physical
- Sexual
- Mental
- Emotional
- Verbal
- Neglect
- Abandonment
- Childhood home abuse
- Alcohol or drug abuse
- Anger
- Violence
- Feeling unsafe
- Single parent
- Absent parent
  - work
  - travel
  - incarceration
  - disinterest
  - divorce
  - death

Shame

Shame is ubiquitous in the human experience. It's practically human nature. Beyond a shadow of a doubt, one
thing I know that you and I have in common is shame. And we
want to have shame. It is not necessarily always a bad thing.
If we didn't have healthy shame, we would all be sociopaths,
and there would be no rule of law. It's the toxic shame that we
can do without.

Since the dawn of time, every culture has used shame to so-
cialize children, form and protect tribes, establish power, and
maintain hierarchy and dominance. We are inherently tribal
creatures, so we need one another. Humans have a deep-seat-

ed longing for belonging and, therefore, a need to please. We are hardwired with an instinctual survival strategy: remain in favor of those who meet our survival needs.

Healthy shame informs us how to behave appropriately, relationally, and situationally. Its purpose and function is to teach us how to thrive in community. Shame molds social mores, which holds communities together. Shame is a vital and necessary part of every society. It is how we learn what our particular culture believes is right and wrong, and good and bad. It is the foundation of manners, etiquette, and social graces. Without healthy shame, there would be no social structure; it would be a chaotic world of 'every man for himself.'

Healthy shame informs us to 'use our inside voice' at white-tablecloth restaurants and to know that we can toss our napkin onto our empty plate at the end of a meal at a greasy-spoon diner. It allows us to express our revelry at a football game differently than we do at church. It should help us behave at an office Christmas party differently than we do at a rave, but there always seems to be that one person who missed the memo.

What is shameful in one group may be lauded in another. Depending on the gathering, you bring forth different parts of yourself and hold other parts back. And then, when you move into a different group, you can bring forward those parts that you held back previously and might even need to pull back the parts that you presented in that other group. It ensures that we can be truly authentic and embrace all of who we truly are and live a more full life, experiencing all kinds of people and cultures. When we have mastery of healthy shame, we can discern how to move from one group to another and feel, the most basic of human needs, a sense of belonging.

Shame is entrenched into the very fibers of our personalities, behaviors, and social engagement. It permeates our conscious and unconscious beliefs about ourselves, others, and the world at large, as well as what we have come to believe others must believe about us.

Shame exists anywhere there is a sense of difference. We generally think of shame as the feeling of being less than, but it can exist whenever we feel unequal to others, even when that lack of equality is in being better than or more privileged.

We are complex and complicated creatures with multifaceted personalities. There are many sides to us and many parts of us. We can enjoy contradictory behaviors and experiences. We can hold two different perspectives of the same dilemma by seeing both sides of the coin.

However, because children can't differentiate between themselves and their behaviors, they come to believe that it is them, not the behavior, that is unacceptable or unwanted. If a child picks her nose and is told that that is gross and to stop doing it, she perceives that she is gross and bad for having done it.

Shame can be used in a way that inhibits play and joyfulness. When children are roughhousing and jubilantly jumping off the furniture and bouncing off the walls, they can be met with, "You kids knock it off! Take it outside!" In a split second, shame can shut down children's exuberance and revelry and plummet them into abject fear and despondency, rendering them into compliance. And in that wounding experience, they might form the belief that it is not okay to be joyful or exuberant.

Millennials suffered from a different kind of shaming: high expectations and accolades, regardless of the level of their accomplishment. Overpraise can be just as damaging and demoralizing as relentless criticism and the expression of disappointment. It's hard to live up to unrealistic expectations and high standards. Shame crept in when they tried really hard and still couldn't make the grade or if they simply didn't have the natural proclivities like being creative or excelling at math. The message remained that there was something wrong with them. The risk of failure or of being found out to be a fraud could lead to a refusal to fully apply themselves. If they didn't try, then they couldn't fail. Participation awards—like when everyone received a trophy just for being a part of the race— lead to a sense of entitlement.

Our brains and nervous systems are hardwired for social engagement. In order to maintain our relationships and therefore survive, we learn that we must not fully be who we really are. Instead, we must change ourselves to become more like the other. It is a survival strategy to deal with a nearly impossible situation: the potential severance of the relationship between oneself and one's caregivers.

Our lives depend on it. We need others to provide us with safety, food, shelter and pleasure. As a way to defend ourselves from feeling the fear of rejection again in the future, we begin to shut down those behaviors or parts of us that are being criticized and begin to self-monitor our thoughts, words, and actions. And, hence, the inner critic is born.

It breeds self-talk like:

- It breeds self-talk like:
- I'm bad.
- I'm wrong or there's something wrong with me.
- I'm broken.
- I'm unfixable.
- I'm unworthy.
- I don't deserve.
- I'm different and not like the others.
- I don't fit in or belong.
- I'm unlovable.
- I always feel left out.
- I'm less than/better than.
- I'm damaged.

Healthy shame, in contrast, sounds more like:

- I'm not perfect, and it's okay.
- I make mistakes, and I learn from them.
- I can do bad things, but that does not make me a bad person.
- I see the value in all parts of me.
- I have the discernment to know which parts of me to bring forward within different groups of people.

I grew up in the House of Shame, halfway between the House of Blues and the House of Pancakes. Like most parents, mine's intentions were good. They didn't mean to damage us; they meant to elevate us. It seemed as though in their minds, my brothers and I were lumps of clay, and, of course, it was their job to create the perfect image to present to the world. So they set out to mold us into who and what they thought would most likely be embraced by others (and reflect positively on their success as parents). But to us, it felt as though all that mattered was meeting their expectations.

Albeit, in hindsight, my parents held themselves to the same exacting standards. We all tend to project our internal experience onto our external world and compare our external environment with our internal environment to try to rectify the two. We simply want to fit in.

Our home, by no means, was bereft of love and affection. Our parents were conscious and conscientious and went well above and beyond the call of duty. They had morals and unquestionable ethics. They did everything in their power to raise us well and properly. They were affectionate and loving. We kissed and hugged our good mornings and good nights, as well as our entrances and exits. They praised our accomplishments. We laughed together. They provided us with an excellent education and many opportunities. We consistently told one another that we loved each other.

And they were detail-oriented perfectionists. No detail was left to chance. They simply wanted us to be the absolute best versions of ourselves as they imagined that we could be. We not only needed to have every hair in place—but there was a place for everything, and everything had to be in its place. We didn't just need to mind our P's and Q's; we needed to mind every letter of the alphabet 24/7/365, 100 percent.

As the youngest of three, I was the low man on the totem pole and under the constant critical judgment of my father, my mother, and both of my brothers. And when you add into the mix my perception of God's wrathful omnipresence, who, like Santa Claus, not only knew when I was being naughty or nice but was privy to all of my thoughts, it felt as though I were squeezed between glass slides under their ever-present watchful eyes peering at me through the long black neck of a microscope.

'You better straighten up and fly right.' When a plane is on autopilot, even though the shortest distance between any two points is a straight line, it is generally off course. Minor adjustments are needed to maintain the trajectory until it lands with pinpoint accuracy. I rarely had a sense of my ultimate destination (because I probably wouldn't have made the right decision anyway), but I was constantly made aware that I was seemingly off course.

I don't want to pretend as if I were the only victim here or that I was an angelic being that was above reproach. We all always seemed to be at one another's throats. It was the culture of our family. None of us knew any differently, and I had assumed all families must have been like that. It was our normal. But, like each of them, I would also crack under the bombardment of personal attacks and defend myself similarly, by tooth and nail and with rapier wit.

It was hard to live up to all of their expectations. As I came to identify with their perceptions of my behaviors, I came to believe that there wasn't anything right or good about me as a person. But, if I could self-police, then I could spare myself some of the pain of being a disappointment in their eyes. To defend myself, I began to micromanage my every thought, word, and action so that they wouldn't be able to. And if I could shame myself out of a behavior, then I could avoid the pain of feeling the shame coming from anyone else. Even my humor became extremely self-deprecating; I tried to sidestep others' criticism of me by beating them to the punch.

When shame is internalized, and we take it on as truth that there is something wrong with us—not just our behaviors—it becomes toxic shame. When we adopt the belief that there is something wrong with our character and begin to identify with ourselves in this way, we spiral into self-loathing and form the belief that we are without value or purpose and, therefore, unlovable. It debilitates us and isolates us from humanity. Toxic shame is like a festering infection that only gets worse over time.

Toxic shame erodes us from the inside out but originates from messaging that we get from the outside world:

- You're a loser.
- You'll never amount to anything.
- I wish you were never born.
- If you don't lose weight, you'll never have a boyfriend.
- You're stupid.
- You're ugly.
- Who do you think you are?
- Don't get too big for your own britches.

- What makes you think that you are so special?
- Have you no shame?
- What's the matter with you?
- How dare you!

In my family, like many others, toxic shame was delivered in humor, chiding, poking fun, criticizing, demoralizing, belittling, diminishing, humiliating, triangulation, shunning, judging, betrayal, and the relentless correction of behavior and points of view. Again, it was death by a thousand paper cuts.

And sometimes shame is expressed nonverbally.

Here are a few examples:

- Side-eyeball glare
- Tsk. Tsk. Tsk.
- Dismissal with a back-handed flip into the air
- Giving someone the middle finger
- Raising of an eyebrow while cocking the head to one side
- Finger-waving
- Turning your back on someone
- Eye-rolling
- Walking away from a conversation

Some believe that shaming is character-building when, in fact, it is the true definition of character assassination. When we learn that there are parts of us that others find undesirable, we begin to police ourselves. We dismember those 'bad' parts of us by suppressing them, silencing them, and trying to kill them off entirely. In essence, we shut down and deny our true selves and our uniqueness.

Toxic shame is the loss of authenticity.

Sometimes, in the developmental stage of individuation, the 'rebellious teenager' tries to re-member some of those lost parts because the internal battle to deny our true nature compels us to reclaim who we truly are. Teens may appear to be rebellious when in truth, they simply need to individuate. But some families and cultures hold steadfast in imposing their limited point of view. In response, some teens acquiesce. But others find environments outside of their homes to explore and express their individuality, free will, autonomy, and natural drives.

When this developmental stage is stunted, there may come the point in time in one's adult life when, no longer under that watchful eye and reprimanding hand of one's family of origin, an internal battle begins between one's higher self and one's inner critic. Sometimes the only chance for those lost parts to survive requires disentangling from the enmeshment, separating oneself from one's own tribe. At times, this is a temporary process for some and for others, it is permanent. It goes against the laws of nature, but so does denial of who we truly are.

The key is to not let shame define us—and the first step is developing awareness.

Awareness of Shame

We simply can't escape shame. However, it is essential to note that while we came into the world with the capacity to feel shame, we did not come into the world in shame. It's not like original sin. Shame originates from external sources. Just because we were shamed, does not mean that we deserved it. Most likely, the shamer is wrong and is to blame for projecting their own internalized toxic shame onto those around them. And it is not always our parents that are to blame. Siblings, teachers, coaches, clergy, and even the media and social media can be the sources of our shame.

Perhaps you might be thinking you don't have any shame. A new client once clarified for me that her problem didn't have anything to do with shame. She said she just had a 'low opinion of herself' and thought she 'deserved all of the difficulties' in her life. She just needed me to help her learn 'how to quit trash-talking herself.' Clearly, she had no understanding of what shame is.

When you are unaware of what shame really is, you certainly won't be able to see how it is pervasive and affects nearly every area of your life. This is unequivocally one of those situations where hindsight is 20/20. I didn't have a clue about how shame was the main player in most, if not all, of the significant issues that I struggled with throughout my whole life. If you are like most of my clients and me, you may never have understood what shame is, much less how it is likely the underpinning of all of your woes. At first, I didn't know how to define it, much less recognize it, but that didn't keep it from running and ruining my life. Shame can be overt and covert.

It is immensely helpful to be able to recognize shame. When I first started studying shame and understood the defense mechanisms or reactions one exhibits when feeling shame, I began to fully see how all-pervasive it is in human behavior. It was similar to buying a new car and then seeing the same make and model more often, or how, once I discovered the defense mechanisms of a narcissist, I became more adept at recognizing them.

The wound of a narcissist is all-pervasive toxic shame. The defenses that the narcissist employs to avoid feeling the pain of shame are, to a great extent, what defines them as a narcissist. I am going to use the following example to illustrate the five primary defense responses that are utilized when one feels shame: deny, attack, fawn, retreat, and self-criticize.

The Five Defense Responses of Shame

Denial is most prevalent through the narcissist's attention-seeking, peacocked-puffery, and the grandiosity they exude. It is not only their attempt to deny that there is something wrong with themselves but to prove to themselves through validation that they are worthy now of getting the attention from others that they most likely did not receive early on in their lives. The searing pain and desperation of the wounds of neglect or abandonment instilled the deepest wound of all: 'I am unlovable.' Even if the parents were present but were disinterested, unavailable, or simply preoccupied—regardless if the preoccupation were warranted, like the parents having to work long hours to keep food on the table or having to prioritize attending to the needs of a chronically ill sibling—the belief that they didn't matter or didn't exist took hold. They may have learned that they had to take extreme measures to be noticed.

Lying, of course, is the denial of truth, regardless of whether one is lying to oneself or to others. It is a way to avoid the pain held within that they are flawed and, therefore, undeserving of love and affection. Denial is also displayed through the rationalizations and justifications for their bad behaviors. Gaslighting is an abject refusal to accept blame. The narcissist will deny and outright lie about what they have said and done (or not said or done) with such voraciousness and finesse that the witness of their abhorrent words and behaviors will call into question their own perceptions.

Attacking others by blame-shifting, projecting their own flaws and faults onto someone else, is an effort to deflect their own and others' focus away from their inherent shortcomings. If they can be the one who points out the flaws in someone else, then they believe that they can distance themselves from others seeing that within them. (Whoever smelt it, dealt it.) It can also be a roundhouse kick to the back of the head of anyone who dares to reflect back to them, even their slightest transgression or foible. This is a one-two punch of denial and attack.

Fawning, sometimes called 'love bombing,' is apparent in excessive and exuberant compliments and displays of affection. It is the initial stage of grooming their prey, an effort to gain their victim's attention or to keep it when it seems to be waning. Fawning is a veiled attempt to prove their value and worth. It is a way to instill the need to be and to remain in a relationship with them. They will go to extraordinary measures, including lavish gifts and promises of a safe and extraordinary future together, to keep anyone in their life which they have been able to win over. Loneliness and solitude are a confirmation of their most basic wound.

The wound of shame is steeped in the terror of the loss of relationships with others. When this threat seems remotely possible, the narcissist, feeling cornered with their back up against the wall, may resort to a last-ditch effort to remain in favor. **Retreat** is an avoidance technique to not continue to feel the pain of potential rejection. This strategy is also a form of manipulation and control. It can be as simple as dismissing the reflection they receive from another by eye-rolling or stonewalling by refusing to carry on a conversation. Or they might make a grand display of how hurt they are in an effort to seek sympathy and empathy to reengage, and thus regain, control. (If you don't want to play with me, then I will take my ball and go home.)

In a narcissist, what seems to be missing within the primary five responses to shame is self-criticism. The shame they feel is so extraordinarily overwhelming; they have honed and mastered their superhero power of denial.

However, **self-criticism** is often the main reaction for anyone who does not have narcissistic wounds and defenses. The criticisms of others have become their reality, and sometimes they even wear it like a badge of honor. They take on the responsibility for and ownership of the shame, believing they deserve it.

When we can identify the defense responses attributed to shame, it can increase our sympathy and patience for others. We can also exercise self-compassion when we are in the throes of our own shame spiral and, consequently, be more empathetic of others, as well.

Unfortunately, merely understanding shame doesn't necessarily mean you will be able to stop your negative self-talk, as it may be through a predominantly cognitive perspective at this time. Gaining mental clarity about how shame works probably won't be enough to motivate you to stick out your hand and introduce yourself when you enter a room full of strangers. Willfully and consciously trying to elevate your thoughts might help to a degree for some time, but it likely won't be enough to stop the habituation.

Rationally, you probably understand that your low self-esteem isn't warranted, but that hasn't changed anything. You think about everything you feel, but you also feel everything you think. If you think badly about yourself, you feel bad. And if you feel bad, then you might think that you are to blame and, therefore, once again, you are bad.

Shame can lead you to undermine your current relationships. Unconsciously fearing that if others were to figure out who you truly were, they wouldn't stick around anyway. It would be best to protect yourself by avoiding closeness. As the loneliness of isolation sets in, your self-loathing can seem so justified that the most logical answer would be to relieve yourself and those around you from the burden of your very existence. Suicidal ideation cannot exist outside of the vacuum of all-pervasive toxic shame.

When we feel we are being seen, heard, gotten, acknowledged, and appreciated, we feel as though we matter. Conversely, when we don't feel those things, we feel like we don't matter. If we find that others are unable to see us as we see ourselves or if they convey that they don't approve of us or judge us for what we say or don't say or do or don't do, then we come to believe that we are wrong, bad, or deficient. If we consistently don't get our needs and desires met, we can come to believe that we must be unworthy of having them met. It is as simple as that.

The Physiology of Shame

It is vital to remember that shame is initially a physiological experience. Shame is felt in the body and is the single worst feeling in the experience of human emotion. Our immediate reaction to being shamed is an intense physiological, non-cognitive defense mechanism to increase the likelihood of being embraced by the shamer, and, therefore, remaining a part of the tribe. Our physiological reaction to shame helps us maintain the interpersonal bridges that are imperative for our survival. During the preverbal, precognitive, and preconceptual stages of early development, rejection and abandonment equate with death. Consequently, this survival reaction cuts a most tender wound to the very core of our existence that rarely heals on its own.

The physiological shame response is a threat response. First, the social engagement system is shut down by breaking eye contact and lowering the head to look down and away as a sign of contrition. Shame's function is to immediately lower affect and reduce the risk of falling out of favor with the care provider. Then the larynx constricts to stop us from saying whatever we are saying. Our bodies become immobilized, either through bracing and constricting the musculature or collapsing into flaccidity. Brain fog sets in, making it difficult to collect our thoughts, much less complete sentences. If we continue to suffer the experience consistently over time, we learn that expressing our emotions, opinions, or perspectives is dangerous. Shame also binds our reactions to old wounds, like grief, to the present moment and influences most of our current thoughts and behaviors.

Shame only recently came into the vernacular when Brené Brown's first TED Talk went viral. As she has shared in many of her talks and books, shame was historically a taboo topic. So much so it's not even mentioned in the curriculum of the study of psychology. She was even warned that it would be career suicide if she continued researching the topic. Thankfully, Brené brought shame out of the closet, as it were.

I have learned so much from her videos, presentations, and writings; however, as a researcher, her conceptualization of shame is primarily focused on the cognitive component, the inner dialogue. However, she certainly conveys the findings of her research in a personal and heartfelt way and clearly identifies the emotional component of shame.

However to some extent, the missing link in her work, is the exploration of the physiology of shame. And again, a physiological wound needs to be addressed physiologically in order to fully heal it.

Let's take a look at the symptoms shame can cause:

- Shyness
- Progress followed by pullback
- Lack of confidence
- Regret
- Social anxiety
- Low self-esteem
- Feeling defeated
- A sense of futility
- Self-sabotage
- Perfectionism
- Fear of incompetence
- Fear of being seen or not heard
- Vicious cycles
- Habituated patterns
- Addictions
- Self-harm
- Eating disorders
- Negative self-talk
- Nausea
- Insomnia
- Lethargy
- Depression
- Immobilization
- Inability to make and hold eye contact
- Paranoia
- Persecution complex
- You feel these symptoms because your inner critic may be telling you:
- There is something

wrong with you.
- You are flawed.
- You are different.
- You are less than or unequal to.
- You are a bad person.
- You can't do anything right.
- You're not worthy.
- You can't ever get it right.
- Perfection is the only option.
- You should be punished.
- You don't deserve well-being, happiness, or success.

Releasing the physiological underpinning of toxic shame by transmuting it into healthy shame restores vibrancy, self-esteem, resilience, and self-reliance. It allows us to return to our authentic selves.

Beliefs and Their Role in Trauma

When I was in boarding school in Vermont, I acquired a beautiful Arabian horse named Huzon. I quickly came to learn that 'Who's-On-And-Let's-See-How-Long-That's-Gonna-Last' would have been a more appropriate name. Huzon could stop on a dime. Whenever he wanted to. Often having found myself being thrown forward, I developed a rather intimate relationship with his thick and majestic neck, clinging on for my life.

Huzon always wanted to remain in the middle of the road. For our safety, I constantly tried to ride along the side of the road. But he just wouldn't have it. Eventually, it became clear that Huzon was terrified of mailboxes on posts that lined the rural roads of the picture-postcard town of Putney. Eventually, I put it together that his former owners had kept him inside a corral with an electric fence. He wasn't afraid of mailboxes; he was scared of the wires that he came to believe were attached to all posts. Had I known then what I know now about threat, instinctual threat responses, and the role of embodied beliefs, I may have been able to help him overcome his conditioned response. But I was resigned to riding in the middle of the picturesque winding roads.

Much of your behavior is learned through the physiological process of stimulus and response. You can learn very quickly that the stove is hot even before you have the mental capacity to understand why it is hot. When you have a wounding experience, like touching a hot stove, you form beliefs about the experience and put into place defenses, coping mechanisms, and survival strategies to protect you in the future from having a similar experience again. In fact, after touching the hot stove once, you may continue to avoid the stove even when it is not hot. Eventually, as cognition and explicit memory comes online, you can discern that the stove is hot when the dial is turned on or when you see the flame or the electric burner is red. Until then, all that matters is to avoid the stove to keep from being burned again. Consequently, your conscious and unconscious beliefs are major players in your early detection warning system.

Over time, those seemingly helpful beliefs can become a double-edged sword. They remain in place until they are challenged (if they ever are challenged), hypervigilant, scanning the horizon for any signs of the possibility of that dangerous experience, ready to do whatever it takes at any moment to prevent that experience from ever happening again.

There may even be a more esoteric law at work—quantum physics and mechanics teaches us, among other things, that we tend to find what we look for. Our beliefs can end up becoming like heat-seeking missiles, actually finding and drawing us toward similar people, places, and things that once wounded us, and, as well as that, they can draw them toward us. Hence, your beliefs create your reenactments, patterns, and habituations.

Beliefs seek validation through confirmation bias. In other words, they can become self-fulfilling prophecies. Many people surrender to them, adopting other beliefs, like, *it's just the way that I am, that's the way the cookie crumbles, life is hard, and it is what it is.*

This is exactly why, regardless of how much knowledge we acquire and how much white-knuckled discipline we exert to break patterns of behaviors, we often still find ourselves repeating the same ol' mistakes. The real culprits in our current-day reenactments are our beliefs. They became hardwired into our physiology.

We have both unconscious, embodied beliefs like these and

cognitive beliefs, which I prefer to call, more appropriately, cognitive convictions. I'm not convinced that a cognitive conviction is indeed a belief. A belief is an original thought that, over time, is affirmed and confirmed through behaviors and experiences until it is habituated. It's an infallible truth that beliefs always win, regardless of our current cognitive convictions or dedication to behavioral changes. This can lead to cognitive dissonance.

Cognitive dissonance occurs when an inherent conflict exists between a mindset or cognitive conviction and an unconscious or embodied belief. An example is when one 'knows better' but continues to carry out behaviors that are not in alignment, like knowing that there isn't a single redeeming quality to smoking tobacco yet maintaining the deadly habit with each flick of a Bic lighter.

It can also be like finding yourself in a depressed mood and not knowing why. Rationally, you can take a look at your life and find that all is well with your relationships, finances, career, etc., so there is no justifiable cause of your sadness—but you feel it nonetheless. Taking a profoundly depressed person to Disneyland, 'the happiest place on earth,' may not have the slightest effect on them if all they see is how everyone else is enjoying themselves and they are not.

Even when we may not be aware of what they are, embodied beliefs always maintain dominance over our cognitive beliefs.

Cognitive dissonance was a way of life for me for so many

years. I couldn't figure out why, regardless of all of the knowledge I had, it wasn't enough for me to sustain changes in behaviors and live in congruence with what I had learned. It seemed that no matter what I did, how intense my lock-jawed determination was, or no matter how much discipline I exerted, I would keep falling into my 'old habits.' It felt as though I would make changes and experience growth and progress, but suddenly 'the Universe' would inexplicably pull the proverbial rug out from underneath me, sending me plummeting back into behaviors and experiences that I was desperately trying to change. Then the shame of feeling like I was so damaged and unfixable would take over, and I would inevitably collapse into futility and give up on all hope that I could be anything or anyone other than who I had been. It just didn't feel like there was any possibility that I could sustain change.

There is a massive difference between a cognitive conviction ('Smoking is bad for me, and I am committed to quit!') and an unconscious embodied belief ('Smoking allows me to feel like a part of a group of people, feel mature beyond my years, and gives me a sense of empowerment and freedom to make decisions that oppose the views of my parents.')

I would like to make a distinction between a belief and a cognitive conviction. A cognitive conviction is just a new thought-form. The idea is that if you repeat a sentence often enough, you will eventually cement it into your consciousness as a new belief, or way of thinking. Thinking about something differently, however, may not equate with a belief. We can choose to think different thoughts that conflict with embodied beliefs or unconscious beliefs, but we are still, nevertheless, holding the original belief—the only difference is that now we also experience the internal conflict of cognitive dissonance.

Beliefs can lie in wait for new cognitive convictions and render them futile without a moment's notice. And as I have established, beliefs always prevail—especially the unconscious ones. Old wounds are over-coupled into a cluster with your beliefs, defenses, and behaviors. This cluster of thoughts and behaviors is influencing you far more than you may be aware of. Not only is this very moment being influenced by your past, but it is also creating your future.

Therefore, the most sure-fire way to change your future is to heal your past, and in doing so, call into question the old beliefs.

So what increases the likelihood of sustainable change? How do we effectively change the beliefs that perpetuate the habituations, patterns, and reenactments of old wounds, once and for all? The answer is simple, but the process in and of itself may not be as easy as we would like to think.

As I mentioned earlier, if our old beliefs are in conflict with a new intellectual conviction, the embodied belief, regardless of whether or not we are even aware of its existence, will undoubtedly prevail. The belief, therefore, is not just in the mind; it is also held in the neurology and biology of the body, imprinted and substantiated through consistent repetitive behaviors. As you are now aware, you cannot heal something in the body by only working with the mind.

"It is easier to behave your way into a new way of thinking than to think your way into a new way of behaving."

- Kegley's Principle of Change

PART FOUR
HEALING

Why We Need to Work With Trauma Somatically

*I*magine your body's nervous system is like a land-mine field of old wounds. You have spent a lifetime unconsciously (or consciously) trying to bury the wounds with dirt, leaves, twigs, and rocks. Some of them you have seemingly managed to forget about. Others you have compartmentalized and ignored. And still others you find yourself in a constant battle trying to keep covered.

Regardless of your efforts, certain people, places, and things apply pressure to the trigger of these old land mines, which makes the wounds resurface. You might not even be cognizant of what the stimuli are; they could be any number of things, like the shape of someone's head, the sound of footsteps, the smell of burnt sugar, or even a certain shade of blue. Certain times of the year or a specific date can set off what is referred to as anniversary trauma. (I know that the winter holiday season brings up a lot in me because I have had family traumas, three significant car wrecks, and have had two major relationships end all within a few days of Christmas.)

When they get triggered and flooded with memories or uncomfortable emotions, most people think that something bad is happening *to* them. Perhaps, in reality, it is something happening *for* them. It just might be an opportunity knocking at the door. It's coming up within you for a reason, because it is the body's way of saying, "Hey, pay attention. There is something here that has not been fully addressed and healed, and now is your opportunity to revisit and renegotiate the old wounds that have just gotten triggered."

When that moment is seized, it can shift into a feeling of empowerment. It's no longer a feeling of 'game over' but rather of 'game time.' You can learn from it and grow as a result of it. You can try to think about it in different ways, to reconceptualize it or spin it in a certain way to give it some kind of new meaning. You can compare the events to other people's experiences to normalizes it. Even better, you also can leverage it as motivation to help create change within yourself or the world.

True profound healing can only occur when we are out of our

comfort zone, not while we are complacently cuddled up cozy on the couch with a cup of chamomile tea. Avoiding or resisting the courageous work simply perpetuates the pattern of unhealed trauma wounds. Covering land mines doesn't get rid of the land mine. Even though you can't change one detail about the reality of what actually happened, it is undeniable that the most challenging times hold the potential to be the most transformative.

Breaking free from your past is no walk in the park. It's an act of courage. Your anger, fear, vulnerability, sadness, and shame have function and purpose. They serve you. They are the sentinels of your learning edges, growth edges, and healing edges. When honored and revered, they will lead you on the hero's journey and return you to vibrancy, vitality, safety, empowerment, and joy. In order to fully feel and embrace the latter, you need to also welcome and explore the former. Read that again. And once more.

HEALING

The Brain's Response to Threat and Trauma

In order to work somatically, you first need to understand some basic neurobiology, which I will do my best to explain in simple, if not oversimplified, terms.

Think of the higher brain as the 'thinker,' the middle brain as the 'feeler,' and the lower brain as the 'behaver' (behavior).

Your higher brain is a marvel. It has many skills and tools available to it, including words, thoughts, and language. It is linear, logical, and rational. It can compare and contrast. Therefore, it is an excellent problem-solver. The problem is that it then needs problems to solve. Because of that, it can be in a constant state of problem-seeking so that it has problems to solve, keeping you in a state of all things problematic, which can, in turn, keep you in a state of worry, angst, and anxiety. It can initiate a state of panic. Your higher brain particularly likes to dredge up problems from the past as well as conceptualize and anticipate all potential problems in the future, even ones that may never come to fruition. Above all, it certainly knows how to hyper-focus on your current problems.

Problem-seeking, problem-solving, rinse, and repeat ad nauseam.

On the one hand, this may be part and parcel of modern man's survival strategy. If you can anticipate potential problems and solve or circumvent them, you will have a problem-free life and a greater chance of survival. However, you end up feeling now what you want to avoid feeling then.

Can you see the problem in that logic? Maybe now you can see why the Buddhists call it the monkey mind. I call it the spin cycle or the crazy maker.

The middle brain function governs emotion, motivation, memory, and image. It is involved in your social engagement. Again, the exact same part of the brain lights up under potential blunt-force trauma (like a baseball bat being swung at your head) as it does under the threat of potential social engagement. It also lights up when you remember a trauma from the past, even if you are currently safe. Threat is threat, regardless if it is perceived or real. It makes sense in that the interactions with people closest to you in your life have, perhaps, even greater capacity to leave longer-lasting wounds than physical wounds that are more likely to heal over time.

In short, the lower brain is a collector of information. The lower brain doesn't understand the difference between perception and reality. It can't differentiate between good and bad or right and wrong. It has to take all the information it collects at face value as if it is real and happening now. It collects information from the higher brain, lower brain, and the five senses. It then mobilizes the autonomic nervous system to react and respond. Historically, the instinctual survival responses have been referred to as the 3 F's: freeze, flight, and fight. As of late, with more scientific research and focus on therapeutic interventions on trauma and instinctual survival mechanisms, two more nuanced F's have become more widely embraced: feign and fawn. At times when the nervous system is completely overwhelmed with threat, the system can completely collapse, and the animal can feign death, like 'possums playing dead.' This phenomenon of employing tonic immobility can also be found in some other mammals, insects, snakes, frogs, and fish as a last-resort defense response. Fawning is an effort to get into the good graces of who or what is threatening you, like pitching food toward an animal that is baring its teeth or when a child negotiates for a lighter punishment, saying, "I'm sorry. I'm sorry! I'll be a good girl. I won't ever do it again."

We are animals, and we have non-cognitive responses to threat and stress (as well as intellectual, emotional, and psy-

chological responses). However, when these instinctual reactions become dysregulated, then no amount of intellectual
understanding or psychological pursuit can restore the system
to equilibrium, homeostasis, and resilience. Please allow me
to repeat myself. It is a physiological problem; it needs to be
addressed physiologically.

To recap, when the higher brain is left to its own devices, it
keeps us in a state of all things problematic. The problem with
that is that the lower brain is then in a constant state of hypervigilance because it assumes that you are under constant
threat. Then the autonomic nervous system responds accordingly, and you will constantly feel the stress of chronic alert in
your body.

The higher brain needs to go offline at night to defrag and
dump its RAM and file folders. But that is not the case for the
lower brain and the autonomic nervous system, which must
be online 24/7 to ensure your safety and well-being. If you are
dead asleep and there is a sound in another part of the house,
or if the door to your room opens and the barometric pressure
of the room changes, or if someone were to sit on the foot of
your bed, it is the lower brain that detects and reacts to the
stimuli.

The lower brain and its governance over the autonomic nervous system (and therefore the felt sense of the body) are the
common denominators of all of our experiences, perceived
and real. It is 'online' and behaving even in the dream realm
when conscious thought appears to be on hiatus. This explains

why, when working with trauma correctly, we don't have to go into every detail of every story. And when there is resolution around one story, there is renewed universal resilience in the nervous system as a whole. Hence healing the wounds around one experience impacts our relationship to the wounds of other stories.

The body's reactions to threat are finite; the mind's reactions are infinite. At times, the lower brain supersedes the higher brain's awareness that threat is present. But the higher brain can override some of the lower brain's defenses.

Clearly we are aware of how emotions and sensations impact the way that we feel physiologically.

Think about some of these colloquialisms:

- Every time she comes around, I get a funny taste in my mouth.
- When I walked into the room, I could feel that the tension was so thick I could cut it with a knife.
- I have a pit in my stomach.
- My stomach is all tied up in knots.
- My stomach is doing backflips.
- He gives me butterflies.
- Going there gives me the heebie-jeebies.
- That guy makes my skin crawl.

Each and every one of the billions and billions of cells in your body, and every system (respiratory, digestive, excretory, musculoskeletal, reproductive, circulatory, nervous, and endocrine), is collectively working as hard as possible to operate at peak efficiency. And like my Latin teacher, Ms. May, taught us on the first day of class, "manus manam lavat" (one hand washes the other), each independent system relies symbiotically on the other. In perfect coherence, the sum is greater than its parts.

When there's so much static going on inside, it's difficult to feel our inner guidance. Intuition is not the voice in the back of your head; its a gut feeling. You can think about anything, as we say in the South, 'a hundred ways from Sunday.' As a result, you can be immobilized and unable to move forward because now you've got 100 choices to choose from. When the system is reorganized and resilient, you can foster an inner knowing, that says, *'It doesn't make sense, but this feels right.'* If you follow that, you will often discover that not only does nothing bad happens, but instead, something good comes of it. And if you do this, you will have a reparative and corrective experience that calls into question an old belief that you tend to make bad decisions.

I had so much fear about being wrong, doing something incorrectly, or making a bad choice that I would defer to others to make the decision. If I were asked where I wanted to go for dinner, I would generally say that it really didn't matter to me. If we had a bad meal, then it wasn't my fault; it was theirs. That's how wily shame can be.

Healing Trauma

*B*t I have intentionally avoided detailing out the intricacies of the aftermath of trauma, like exploring all of the symptoms and ramifications of PTSD, anxiety, and panic. I want this book to focus more on the root causes of your suffering than on the presentations of your struggles. I imagine that you are more than aware of how all of it has been playing out for you.

And I hope that what you discover in reading this book will encourage you to find support. Successfully healing trauma and the trauma of shame requires a practitioner who has mastered specific skills to reduce the risk of re-traumatization.

And when you do, you will be in a much better position to put them to work for you to fast-track your progress. There are different modalities available, some more effective than others, and some that are counterproductive or even contra-indicated.

At times, I have had clients who showed up for their first session ready to rumba, but more oftent than not, we had to build the toolbox and practice the necessary skills before we entered into the trauma vortex. We have a few axioms in working with trauma and shame: Less is more. Slower is faster. Resource, resource, resource.

Developmental trauma and shame are relational wounds. So restoring healthy relational attachment is most effective when explored within the context of a current healthy relationship. It is paramount that you feel safe and trust the therapeutic alliance with your practitioner.

Healing shock trauma also requires re-establishing a sense of safety and trust, but more specifically within your body and your envirionment. Circumventing habituated ingrained de-fenses and coping strategies on your own may prove to be challenging, even if you have the conscious awareness of what they are. But the good news is, when you are working with a practitioner, who knows how to work with shock traumas and your unnique defense structures, you won't be spinning your wheels or wasting time.

Regardless, its different for each person and takes time. But you will get better results in less time than if you try to do it on your own, or only through the use of books, spiritual practices, behavioral changes, courses, and non-trauma-informed support.

I had had the honor to study directly with Dr. Levine when I did my advanced training in Brazil. And over the years, I have assisted both Maggie Kline and Abi Blakeslee, faculty at Somatic Experiencing International, in several trainings for Somatic Experiencing practitioners as part of the three-year training program.

One thing I have learned over the years is that everybody has a story. Nearly everyone has endured some sort of heinousness that changed them at their core. It seems nearly impossible to navigate life on planet Earth and remain unscathed. At times, I could not understand how the person sitting across from me had survived the kinds of atrocities that seemed completely implausible and possibly insurmountable. But, having worked in this field for nearly two decades, I have witnessed travesties transform into triumphs.

Healing trauma is different from managing symptoms. Managing and mitigating symptoms may bring a sense of relief. Temporarily. Until the original wounds of trauma are explored and worked with somatically, you will find yourself in an endless search for new and additional ways to deal with your uncomfortable feelings, unshakeable beliefs, habituated behaviors, and those ever-present aggravating symptoms.

As I have mentioned previously, many people are habituated in denying, ignoring, disconnecting, suppressing, and distracting themselves from their bodies in general and, thereby, from the sensations in their bodies. So, if they have habituated behaviors, including cognitive rationalization and explanation, to get themselves out of or away from what they feel—then they may have created a maladaptive defense that inhibits their ability to truly heal.

If someone doesn't feel anger, sadness, fear, vulnerability, or shame, it does not necessarily mean that those emotions aren't present. It might be that, over an extended period of time, they have repressed their uncomfortable sensations and feelings and found creative ways to redirect their attention. Instead, they might experience flatness, numbness, futility, despondency, disconnectedness, chronic tiredness, anxiety, panic, or dissociation.

And, I can only imagine, you wouldn't want to live flatlined any more than you would like to be in a perpetual state of hyperarousal. Our neurobiology and physiology are designed to be expressive. We live in a polarized Universe within the juxtaposition of opposites, but it is not a world of black and white. We can only gain perspective through experiencing all of the shades of gray.

To review the Gendlin research, the single most determining factor as to whether or not anyone gets better in any practice with any practitioner is based on the client's ability to feel sensations in their bodies, express those sensations appropriately through language, and then attach the right affect and meaning to that experience. There is the inclusion of cognitive processes—thought, language, and meaning—but it begins at the rudimentary level of bodily sensations and our ability to feel them.

Although the body's reaction to threat is relatively consistent, there are variables in the approach to how to work with them. In the Somatic Experiencing training, we spend three years in a deep dive, exploring how to work with all different kinds of threats (stimuli) and the nuanced ways the body reacts (responses). Trauma occurs because the system experiences too much all at once or not enough over time. A car wreck is an example of too much all at once, and abandonment is an example of not enough over time. We study the neurobiology of how the body-mind connection can become disorganized or stuck due to highly arousing (overwhelming) events or collapse in response to underwhelm. And, of course, we learn the most effective ways to help the client safely reengage with old wounds and support them while the body renegotiates the event physiologically. Working with loss requires a different approach than working with an accident. Working with someone stuck in hypervigilance requires a different approach than someone who is chronically dissociated, like depersonalization.

The narrative is used but only as a catalyst to bring the body's reactive memory back online and only just enough for the client to tolerate that part of the memory they are reliving. The sequence of the narrative is generally worked with out of order to avoid re-traumatizing the system, and we slow things down by only exploring one little moment at a time. Because the lower brain (reptilian brain) cannot distinguish perception from reality, the lower brain reacts as if it is happening again when we have an implicit or explicit memory. That is why we have emotional reactions to our memories. And remember, emotion is the felt sense experience of a collection of sensations, neurochemicals, micro-movements, and gross behaviors.

The Somatic Experiencing practitioner's objective is to safely stimulate the client's nervous system into a tolerable level of activation—the physiological expression of sensation—then encourage the nervous system to discharge so that it can reorganize and return to resilience. Within resilience is an expansion of the client's banks of toleration. It is also crucial for the practitioner to share practical resources, skills, and tools so that the client is better equipped to handle future threats and stressors. In doing so, the client moves toward greater self-containment and, ultimately, self-reliance.

A Somatic Experiencing session is an educational and experiential process, which should also include learning new skill sets. Much time and attention are spent getting the client resourced (feeling better). Discovering how and why the body reacts the way it does when facing threat combined with applying the aforementioned skill sets help to recondition and reinstate orienting responses, healthy boundaries, safety, healthy aggression, and joyfulness.

Again, the lower brain doesn't know the difference between what is real and what is perceived, which is how we can be traumatized by horror, witnessing terrible things that happen to other people, or re-traumatized from flashbacks. So if the perception of or memory of danger can traumatize, we can also use the imaginal realm to facilitate healing, as long as the felt sense is part of the process. For example, you can notice what happens in the body in the current moment as you re-imagine the details of an event, help arriving sooner or an entirely different outcome.

Touch can also be incorporated to resource the client with a sense of support and increase attention and connection to sensation as well as with the body itself in general. Consciously attuned touch can also stimulate or trigger old wounds. Applied, skilled technique can help the body renegotiate and release old holding patterns and truncated physiological defense mechanisms.

For example, if touch feels unsafe for a client, the practitioner might begin to reestablish safe touch simply by making contact with one of their feet by placing it next to the client's foot. The initial contact could cause arousal in the nervous system within the client. At that point, they are encouraged to feel into (in other words, pay attention to what they are feeling) the internal alarm until it begins to settle. If it is too arousing, the client can be empowered to request that the practitioner stop touching them and perhaps even ask them to move away. The client is in control, which, ideally, restores confidence and a sense of empowerment.

Remember, even if you know what needs to be healed, old limiting beliefs, outdated defense mechanisms, and coping strategies still may be at play. That which once helped you manage a difficult experience, more than likely over time, has become maladaptive and detrimental, perhaps even further compounding your problems. In fact, these antiquated defense structures may literally keep you from being able to even gain access to the original wound. And they could be what inhibits you from being able to sustain long-lasting changes.

For example, the client who feels unsafe being touched might be sexually promiscuous. They might be subconsciously trying to normalize sex by having a series of one-night stands. However, in doing so, they are avoiding sensuality or real intimacy. This could result in the person feeling a sense of freedom and empowerment by being dominant sexually, but cringing when someone looks lovingly into their eyes while caressing the back of their hand.

A resilient nervous system is quite expressive and allows us to feel a full spectrum of bodily sensations and emotions, both for pleasure and to bring awareness to threat and distress. When the nervous system is not in a state of high arousal nor collapsed into immobility, it affects the way that we feel, just as it affects how we feel when it is in a state of arousal or in a non-reactive state. Many people find the sentient experience of constant arousal uncomfortable and alarming, and the sentient experience of not feeling anything can be just troubling to others.

Exposure therapies based on desensitization concern me to some degree. The client is encouraged to relive memories and repeat their stories ad nauseam. The result may very well be a reduction in the expression of their symptoms, but at what cost? If the beliefs formed as a result of the original wounding experience are still in place, then habituated behaviors and vicious cycles will likely continue. But now they may not have access to the feelings they need to feel to fully discharge the nervous system, reducing the likelihood that they will be able to break the patterns.

The good news is that effectively healing trauma physiologi-cally is non-linear. Resolution around one story or event can have a global impact. While I was going through my personal process with my Somatic Experiencing practitioner, Beverly Buehner, I noticed my relationships changing, even though I hadn't dealt with my relationships in the sessions yet. The only thing that we had worked on were the events of my car wreck.

But how could that be? Because I was changing. I was less on guard and reactive. People couldn't push my buttons the way they once had because my alert response had finally begun to settle after having been previously stuck in hypervigilance. My relationship with myself and the world changed because I felt differently with a more resilient nervous system. I was showing up in the details and circumstances of my life in a new, better, different, and even novel way.

And now you have now come to learn that you can't change your past, but you can change your relationship to it. You can leverage it. You can shift the way you respond to it and lean in and get curious and willing to feel the feelings, and by doing so, you can truly heal.

If you have been disappointed with your progress before, using a method that wasn't the best approach, then you may have more resistance now, even when you are on the right path. Keep your attention focused on positive shifts and changes, especially the subtle ones, even if they seem unrelated to the material that you are focusing on.

Neuroplasticity and its Role in Trauma

The brain has the capacity to change at any point in our lives, and we have the ability to influence our brains to change. Just like our brains are negatively influenced by what I have referred to as death by a thousand paper cuts—repetitive micro-aggressions, shaming experiences, or neglect—the brain can also be influenced positively to create new neural pathways of positive thoughts, healthy behaviors, and more desirable emotional states.

In part, the physiological changes that occur as a result of healing trauma are an example of neuroplasticity. We can facilitate neural pathways to change and how we have come to think and behave to change as well. We can reorganize former neural pathways and/or create new neural pathways.

Most people and many healing modalities try to change the reality of the details and circumstances of the external environment in an effort to change the internal environment, or how they are feeling. But when instead, we change the reality of the internal experience, then the ways that we think, feel, and behave change naturally. This, in turn, changes how we experience and engage with the external environment. So the external environment reflects the internal environment rather than the other way around.

Healing trauma does not have to be entirely painful and arduous; in fact, it might even be more effective, quicker, and longer-lasting when interspersed with curiosity, play, and laughter. Dr. Caroline Leaf, a pioneer in neuroplasticity research, the study of how the brain can change, is the author of *Cleaning Up Your Mental Mess*. According to Dr. Leaf, it requires 400 repetitions to create a new synapse in the brain. However, when consciously directed thoughts or behaviors are introduced via play, the number of repetitions needed can be reduced to as few as 40. This also explains how the use of the imaginal realm can be highly impactful in healing old wounds. Play, curiosity, celebration, reward, and the imaginal realm are dopamine-rich experiences. And Dr. Leaf explains that dopamine is the jet fuel of neuroplasticity.

I do my best to bring humor and levity into my sessions, if and when appropriate. I always invite my clients to play with the tools, exercises, and skills I share. And one of the reasons why I say, 'play--don't 'practice' is that practice can move us into the shame spiral of perfectionism. On the other hand, when we are in a playful frame of mind, we enter into curiosity. Curiosity moves a human being out of inertia, out of stillness, and into behavior. We also think that curiosity is the opposite of shame because shame is a frozen state, and curiosity is an inquisitive state. Social engagement requires curious inquiry.

HEALING

Original Wounds

Typically, when we think of wounds, we think of broken bones, cuts, and scrapes. These wounds are generally short-lived and self-regenerative. The body's innate capacity to heal is nothing short of miraculous and mind-boggling. But wounds can also be psychological and emotional, perhaps even spiritual. And those seem to be the hardest to heal, oftentimes continuing to impact the quality of our lives for the rest of our lives.

Dr. Levine compares the nervous system to a river. The energy in the nervous system is like the flowing water. The banks of the river contain the water and direct the flow. If a boulder (threat) drops into the river, the impact displaces the water (response), which breaches the riverbank (the nervous system's bank of toleration). The boulder not only disorganizes the water but scars the riverbed and forever impedes the normal flow. It remains in place like a newly formed belief.

Words are powerful. The judgment and criticism we receive from others can be more painful and damaging than actual physical harm. The scars they leave and the beliefs that we form as a result can continue to wreak havoc for years.

Some would say that verbal abuse is psychological abuse because the words we hear engage our cognition to make sense of them and understand their meaning. But the meaning of words and our interpretation of them create a physiological response in the body. (We feel everything we think; we think about everything we feel.) The terror that we feel from the impact of the criticism is the fear of rejection, the breaking of the interpersonal bridge, or, in other words, the loss of the relationship. From a child's perspective, that has life-or-death consequences, as we are entirely dependent upon the care of others for our survival.

"I brought you into this world, and I can take you out!"

"And this is why I never wanted children."

"You're stupid."

"You're never going to amount to anything."

When I was 18, I had a coworker tell me that when I smiled, 'it ruined my whole face.' You can only imagine how that impacted me and my life for years to come.

From a trauma perspective, an original wound is any physiologically dysregulating experience that remains unresolved. Unresolved wounds are disorganized or stuck energy in the nervous system. The reason they go unresolved is generally due to the fact that at the time, we had limited life experience and lacked the necessary support, resources, and intellect to properly cope with overwhelm or underwhelm.

It is imperative that we not just compartmentalize the past. Instead, we need to become willing to excavate old wounds in order to truly heal them, but it's not just a matter of revisiting the hurt and wallowing around in it. That's not healing. In fact, it is more likely to be re-traumatizing. And, I'm not saying that you can't change without healing your past. But it is, however, infinitely easier when you don't have to fight against old limiting beliefs that you formed at the time of the wounding experiences.

Again, these beliefs can change how we think about ourselves, other people, certain behaviors, environments, or events. The belief is there to help protect us if we were to ever encounter a similar situation or person in the future. But the belief is a double-edged sword. On the one hand, it is constantly scanning the horizon for the potential of a reenactment, but it can also draw us toward reenactments—and draw reenactments toward us.

Birds of a feather flock together. Energy attracts like energy. Water finds its own level. And beliefs always win. No matter how strongly convicted we are, how much discipline we leverage, or how fervently we work to change the way we think and behave, our beliefs remain victorious through confirmation bias.

Part of what I do with my clients is help them recognize when they're in the midst of a reenactment so we can search for the original wound. More often than not, the way the client is currently feeling in their present circumstances is similar to how they felt during the original wounding experience. At that point, we're working with the same energy: the energy of the nervous system that has been desperately trying to discharge, reorganize, and return to equilibrium.

So how do we heal these original wounds and stop the reenactments? First of all, we have to recognize that reenactment is an opportunity. When facing yet again the same old story, most people move into action to deal with the current circumstances, thinking that if they can fix the problem or change the details and circumstances, they will feel better. They think that if they can just get through this latest ordeal, they can return to life as usual.

However, even if they solve the current problem, the old wound is still standing in the wings, flailing its arms about and screaming, "What about me?!? Can you deal with me now? Do you have the skills, tools, resources, intellect, or support now?"

But all too often, it goes unnoticed, or its screams fall on the deaf ears of denial. So the old wound thinks to itself, *I guess not. But, I'll be back. Okay? I'll try ya again later. Don't you worry, I'll find another situation in the future and try to say 'hello' again. Maybe then you'll be ready.*

Most people don't know how to look for the original wound and often avoid doing so. Consequently, they miss the opportunity to address it and break the chain. Anytime you behave or react disproportionately to a current event in your life, it is usually indicative that the historical charge in your nervous system is compounding the response you are having to the present circumstances. Recognizing this can help lead you to the original wound.

Healing Toxic Shame

Healing toxic shame is a bit of a misnomer. We don't want to heal it; we want to transmute toxic shame into healthy shame. Healthy shame enables us to accept our imperfections and still feel as though we are amazing. My favorite new word is an amalgamation of flawed and awesome. It is time that we all step into the perfectly imperfect wholeness of being 'flawesome.' I long for the day when flawesome is no longer underscored by spell check. (Autocorrect has become my own worst enema—er, enemy!)

You make mistakes. We all do. And we can learn from them.

You occasionally say or do stupid things, but that doesn't mean you are stupid. You say or do unkind things, perhaps (rarely) even intentionally, but that doesn't make you a mean person. You may say things in certain circumstances that land in others as hateful, but that does not mean you are an unloving person.

Toxic shame resides in the identification with your limiting beliefs about your Self. Healthy shame thrives in the awareness that you are not perfect, that you can make mistakes, and that sometimes there is a difference between your behavior and character. Neither your thoughts nor your behavior defines you, but they are expressions of different parts of you. Sometimes a part of us can become so dominant it takes over as if it is our identity.

Personally, healing toxic shame has been the single most transformative journey of my entire lifetime. It has informed and increased my capacity exponentially to help others heal. But it wasn't until 12 years into my private practice that I stumbled upon a webinar about healing shame with Bret Lyon and Sheila Rubin from The Center for Healing Shame. Although I had been aware of Brené Brown's influential first TED Talk, *The Power of Vulnerability* (now with more than 17,000,000 views), I really didn't have any understanding about healing shame.

When I listened to the webinar, I had what I call a 'Hellen Keller moment.' I recall as a child watching *The Miracle Worker*, starring Anne Bancroft and Patty Duke Astin, now known as Patty Duke. There is the seminal moment in the Academy Award-winning film when Hellen Keller, a blind, deaf, and mute child, is finally able to make the connection between the hand signal gestures that Anne Sullivan has been trying to teach her with the words 'water' and 'mother.' In that revelation, Helen's world opened up like Forrest Gump's box of chocolates. I suddenly had the language and basic understanding of the deepest layer of my own wounding, beliefs that I held about myself and what I had come to believe that others believed about me, and I began to conceptualize how pervasive shame had been in my life.

I immediately signed up for the next live training at The Center for Healing Shame in Berkeley, California. Not only did I complete the certification, I told Bret and Sheila that they needed an assistant and that it was going to be me. At my own time and expense, over the next four-plus years, I continued to fly to Berkeley nearly every single month, attending all but five of the trainings. Unfortunately, my dream to carry on their legacy and teach their work did not come to fruition for various reasons.

Shame is the linchpin of our oldest, deepest, and most impactful wounds. Healing shame is the most transformative of all healing. When we transmute our toxic shame into healthy shame, everything changes within the deepest core of who we are and, consequently, how we engage with and are embraced by others.

Society may reject us if we don't have healthy shame and behave accordingly, but we may remove ourselves from society if we become imprisoned by all-pervasive toxic shame. Even though the underlying fear in feeling shame is the fear of re-jection and isolation, it is also, at times, a choice we need to make in order to protect ourselves from feeling more shame. Isolation is the worst punishment we put human beings through, save the death penalty. And, yet, feeling shame is so inexplicably painful we will reject others and choose to isolate ourselves.

Shame drives both perfectionism and self-sabotage. If you had come to believe that you were a disappointment to your loved ones because they never seemed satisfied or expressed that they were proud of you, then no wonder you would relent-lessly attempt to be the example of what you believed would please them. Perfectionism is a learned behavior. It is an effort to flawlessly meet the needs and desires of others so that you can prove that you have value and worth.

When facing unrealistic expectations, fear of failure breeds anxiety. Fear of making a single mistake can lead to immobi-lization, which can then amplify the anxiety into panic. How could you move forward if you don't know beyond a shadow of a doubt what the next best move would be? It's like needing to go to the grocery store, but sitting in the driveway waiting for all the traffic lights to turn green first.

Worrying that you will fall short of your own standards may very well awaken the beast of self-sabotage. And, sometimes, even when you beat the odds, gain some momentum and re-alize some changes, the underlying belief remains that you are unworthy and undeserving of your accomplishments. So, to avoid being found out or called to the mat for being a fraud, perhaps it would be prudent to not take a risk, like asking your boss for that raise that is long overdue. Your higher brain tends to fixate on what is wrong or problematic, so if you fall short of expectations, that will remain your focus, thereby diminishing or discounting all the progress you made along the way.

In the therapeutic process, when a client can't seem to get better or has a tendency to backslide following progress, it's most likely that shame is to blame. There may be a conscious or unconscious belief that they don't deserve to get better or to feel good.

The early developmental wounds of toxic shame, the beliefs formed around them, and the defenses you developed over time are both a quagmire and a labyrinth. Negotiating through the morass is nearly impossible without the proper skilled support. Since shame is predominantly an instinctual physiological survival mechanism to a relational quandary, it must also be effectively worked with physiologically and inter-relationally.

The journey begins with learning to recognize shame in all its forms, which is easier to do when it is overt but may require expertise to tease it to the surface when it is covert. And being able to see it for what it is is only the first step in the process. Understanding that it wasn't your fault and that there wasn't anything inherently wrong with you is a big step in the right direction.

Toxic shame takes hold when you subjugate yourself to accepting other people's opinions of you as facts, believing that their limited experience of you is more accurate than the cumulative expression of all that you are. When you can clearly see shame in all of its forms, bringing toxic shame into the light of your conscious awareness, then you have already begun the process of transmuting it into healthy shame. Healthy shame helps you to determine that other people's opinions matter and should be taken into consideration, but you get to determine how much of others' opinions matter and whether or not other people's opinions are incongruous with how you see yourself.

Once you can identify and properly name it for what it is, you can begin to gain optimal distance from it. Instead of being fully engrossed in its web of lies, you can begin to witness it and feel the shame from this new perspective. You will start to shift how you had internalized it to the point that it became a part of your identity.

When you can sense how and where you feel the shame in your body, you may begin to recognize how it does not feel like it is yours or even 'of you,' but it is held within you. You took on other people's opinions of you as if they were correct in their observation, and you then took ownership of what you came to believe was wrong or bad about you. But oftentimes, it wasn't that there was something wrong with you. There was, in fact, something wrong with them. It was the shamer's lack of agency and capacity to embrace what you were saying or doing (or not saying or doing) at the time. The truth of your expression triggered the wounds or limitations of the person who shamed you, which is a greater reflection of them than it is of you. More likely than not, they were the adults in the room, and you were simply a child acting like a child.

Releasing the physiological underpinning of toxic shame by transmuting it into healthy shame allows us to return to the wholeness of our true authentic selves. To do this, we must *re-member* those parts of us that we dis-membered earlier in life, reclaiming our lost, abandoned, and denied parts. We need to expand the current container of *who we are now* to be able to hold all parts of us once again. Not only will you feel more comfortable in your own skin, but you will also discover and embody an unshakeable sense of *all that you truly are.*

Shame and its Role in Anger

I would be remiss if I didn't talk specifically about the relationship between shame and anger. In toxic shame, the two are fused together like conjoined twins.

Three things are ever-present in clinical depression and suicidal ideation besides sadness: all-pervasive toxic shame, futility (the hopelessness of, *Why bother? What's the point?*), and unexpressed anger. As I mentioned in the chapter Nitty-Gritty, sadness and anger can be twin flames. In depression, the external expression of sadness is most prevalent, while anger is more often directed inward. When I work with depression, suicidal ideation, and toxic shame, I prioritize helping my client to explore their relationship with anger.

There is a Buddhist expression, "Holding on to anger is like swallowing poison and expecting the other person to die."

As I have mentioned before, we live in a polarized Universe, so even our emotions have polarity. The most extreme form of anger is harm of self or harm of others, as in suicidal ideation and homicidal rage. Consequently, it stands to reason that on the opposite end of the spectrum of anger is care of self and care of others, as in self-preservation and protection of others. In between the two polarities exist dozens of affects, like disappointment, frustration, annoyance, and disgust, just to name a few. Anger is a vital and necessary energy; it is part of our life force. It has value and purpose and serves us well. Without it, we lack agency and self-confidence.

Wait. What? Anger is part of self-confidence? Allow me to explain.

In order to self-preserve, you need to have healthy boundaries, and healthy aggression (the positive polarity of anger) is necessary to establish and protect those boundaries. Boundaries are either physical, like the boundary of your skin, or energetic, like the boundary of time. Energetic boundaries are determined by your personal perspective of what is right and wrong for you: what you think is good or bad, what you like and what you don't like, what you value and what you don't value, what matters to you and what doesn't matter to you, etc. In short, healthy boundaries are your 'yeses and noes.'

If you want to self-preserve and live a longer and more ac-tive life by adopting a healthy lifestyle, you will need to be able to set healthy boundaries for yourself. You will need to set a boundary around making the time to work out, and you will need to protect that boundary by not allowing anything or anyone to interfere with your workout schedule. You will also need to set boundaries about what you will eat and won't eat. If you are able to set and protect these boundaries, then you have what is referred to as 'discipline.' So you need healthy aggression to have discipline. If you have discipline, then you also have drive, ambition, chutzpah, get-up-and-go, vim and vigor, vitality, vibrancy, inner strength, and self-empower-ment. If you have all of that, then you have the building blocks for self-esteem and self-confidence.

So in order to have self-confidence, you need to have healthy aggression. Self-confidence is derived from being so self-as-sured that your North Star is what matters to you. Hence, you are so comfortable in your own skin and resolute in your perspectives that other people's opinions of you simply don't matter—they are perfectly entitled to their opinions, but you don't take them on as if there is something wrong with you for thinking, feeling, or behaving differently than they do. So, yes, healthy aggression is the foundation of self-confidence.

On the other hand, when you lack self-esteem or are insecure, there is almost always an inhibition around feeling anger and expressing it. That can lead to having no boundaries or fuzzy boundaries. Consequently, you generally abandon your true authentic Self and adopt other people's perspectives as your own, kowtowing to the others' needs and demands.

It is quite common for all-pervasive toxic shame to inhibit the expression of anger externally. When anger is not expressed externally, it is expressed internally. One of the main physiological shame responses is to quickly lower affect or emotional expression. Shame binds to, and is the underpinning of, most emotions, especially anger. After a lifetime of being shamed for having anger and expressing it, the anger is redirected inward onto oneself. And anger toward oneself leads to self-sabotage and self harm.

The fear in expressing anger is the fear of annihilation. You may have come to learn that when you expressed your anger, it hurt someone. The shame you felt in hurting someone drives the belief that you were bad or wrong for doing so.

But what happens most often when children express their anger is that they are met with an overwhelming amount of anger in return or corporal punishment, like a slap across the face. Or they are shunned—ignored, put in the corner for a 'time out,' or sent to their room—with shaming declarations like:

"How dare you! Who do you think you are, speaking to me like that?"

"I don't know what I did to deserve having such an ungrateful brat!"

"You shut your mouth, or I'm going to hit you so hard you will wake up in the middle of next week!"

It is important to note that even though the parent may have exercised restraint (by resisting physical violence) in these verbal examples, shunning can instill an unconscious belief within the child that they don't matter or don't even exist. And as a defense against this, they will likely learn to fawn and 'people-please' to prove that they have value and worth. At the very least, they will learn that they are not allowed to have anger or express it.

Changing Beliefs

I refer to myself as a stress and trauma specialist, but in reality, I ultimately help people change their beliefs. However, I rarely specifically work on getting my clients to change their beliefs. Of course, I may inquire if the client has an any idea of what beliefs they may be aware of that are holding them back for a point of reference. Still, the beliefs change on their own when the original wounds are healed and the client has enough corrective and reparative experiences in their current everyday life to call into question the validity of their limiting beliefs.

As I have mentioned before, beliefs are the deepest layer underneath so many of your behaviors. You can have unconscious embodied beliefs and conscious beliefs (cognitive constructs). Unconscious beliefs, or subconscious beliefs, may have been formed when you were preverbal, precognitive, and preconceptual before you even had the neurobiology of cognitive memory. Embodied memory is a part of your survival instincts, and so they are designed to last a lifetime to protect you and keep you safe. They may have served you during the time in your life when they were vitally important, but over time they may have become maladaptive and detrimental. They no longer serve you; they harm you. They keep you stuck in patterns and habituations, refusing to let you fully mature. And they can get in the way of the healing process of changing conscious beliefs.

You might be asking yourself now, "If I have no conscious memory of the wounding experience or any awareness of the beliefs that I formed as a result, then how could I possibly fully heal?"

Embodied beliefs present as feelings, or a collection of sensations, in the body. When I can assist a client to become willing to feel what they are feeling (how and where in their body are they feeling what) and I can help them to tolerate and remain in that sentient experience long enough, I then ask if there is anything old and familiar about the way they are feeling. More often than not, images, thoughts, or memories begin to surface in their conscious awareness. But sometimes, when there is no conscious memory, it is most likely an unconscious embodied memory. By tracking the current arousal in the nervous system, we have gained access to the physiology of the felt sense arousal of the original wound being held in the nervous system. Now, I can use the tools and techniques of Somatic Experiencing to encourage the nervous system arousal to unwind, releasing the dysregulation. Once the dysregulation discharges, the nervous system is able to self-regulate, reorganize, and return to equilibrium or greater resilience. In essence, the client's body has had a reparative and corrective experience. The stuckness of the old holding pattern, perhaps a truncated defense response, is released. If at the same time, we're also able to replace the old defenses with more effective ones and new ways and means of self-soothing and self-regulating, we can break the pattern entirely and a new belief can be formed—the belief that it is now currently safe for them to be in their body and in the world.

Your conscious beliefs may tell you that you have already tried everything to heal and nothing has worked, so you are unfixable. You have acquiesced to the false reality that you are damaged and broken beyond repair. You may have adopted all the rationalizations and justifications that you are so intrinsically different; you don't fit in anywhere, and, therefore, you are unlikeable and unloveable. You may have come to believe that you are just the way you are, and your dreams of greatness are just delusions of grandeur.

Many people think that what they need to do to change a behavior is to change their thinking. Indeed, we can change a thought and choose a different behavior, like, *Smoking is bad for my health, and I don't want to smoke this cigarette, so I am not going to light it,* and then choose to return it to the pack. But the thought alone did not effectuate the change. They also had to carry out the behavior. They lived in the clutches of cognitive dissonance and the internal conflict they felt but continued to carry on the behavior. The cognitive conviction alone that smoking was bad for their health was not enough to change the behavior.

Again, many people also think that in order to change a belief, all they need to do is change their minds. They think that if they can catch a negative belief and reframe it into a positive belief, then eventually they won't have the negative belief anymore. That is true to some degree if habituated enough times through repetition. But if they held and repeated that prior negative belief consistently for decades, how many repetitions of the new desirable belief would it take to transform it? And, as I have previously postulated, our beliefs are the foundation of much of our behavior. Therefore, a cognitive conviction, alone, isn't enough to change a belief.

But if they were to catch the negative belief and then immediately act upon the new positive thought that they want to be healthier—like crushing the unlit cigarette while feeling a sense of empowerment in choosing a healthier lifestyle—then it stands to reason that they would free themselves of the old belief much more quickly. And they could speed up the process if, each time they crushed an unlit cigarette, they celebrated themselves with a happy dance or gave themselves a pat on the back, giving themselves a hit of dopamine.

Again, thinking and behaving differently in an effort to change beliefs is only part of the equation. And you have learned now that to fast-track the process, reduce the likelihood of old patterns resurfacing, and ensure personal transformation, it is necessary to actually heal the original wounds that set up the habituations in the first place. If the drive to smoke originated from feeling as though you didn't fit in anywhere, but you found that you could fit in when you lit up with other smokers, then those beliefs can be called into question consciously each time you have a pleasant social encounter with someone who doesn't smoke.

On a side note—it is crucial to take into consideration that some habits, like smoking tobacco, also have a physiological addiction component that can trump all other efforts. Even after you heal the original wound and change your beliefs that you have unconsciously held about smoking, you will still have to muscle through the physiological withdrawal.

The uncomfortable sensations of withdrawal, if not worked with properly, may very well undermine all of your other efforts and progress. Your body has become so dependent on nicotine, it is begging for more, just like hunger is the body's way of begging for food. However, if you can remember that what you feel as your body craves nicotine is tolerable, and you don't need to go to the emergency room, you can move into empowerment. In that place of empowerment, you can become willing to lean in and feel the individual sensations one by one. By doing so, you will reduce the resistance that you have to feeling the sensations and decrease their power over you. While focusing on the feelings, remind yourself that you are choosing to live a healthier lifestyle and are willing to experience the temporary discomfort for the long-term gains.

Eventually, the body will begin to repair and reorganize without the nicotine and no longer crave it. In fact, that is happening simultaneously. So, you can even tell yourself that what you are feeling is your body repairing and healing itself. And each time the cravings pass, and you crush the unlit cigarette—pat yourself on the back, give yourself a fist bump, do some jumping jacks, or run in place. Then tell yourself how proud you are of yourself and that you are a champion—you won that battle in the long, arduous war over one of the most addictive substances known to man. Now throw your arms in the air with your hands in fists and hold the victory stance for a few moments with a great big ol' smile plastered onto your face. You did it! You deserve it.

The Neuroplasticity of Beliefs

We have two kinds of thoughts. We have errant thoughts that seemingly come out of nowhere, and we also have the ability to think. When thoughts come into our awareness, we can witness the thoughts and then critically think about those thoughts.

And whenever we have a thought bubble up out of nowhere, we can rightfully assume that it is seeking our attention. If we pay attention to it and contemplate it, we are listening to our thoughts. Then, depending upon the meaning that the thought has for us, the nervous system responds by creating sensations in the body to command even more of our attention. Remember, the lower brain collects information from our thoughts, and it can't differentiate a thought from reality. But the thought only becomes a part of our reality when the lower brain interprets it as real and alerts the nervous system to respond to it, hence we feel what we think. But until then, it is just a thought.

However, it is a two-way street since we can also think about everything we feel. So when we feel a sensation, the higher brain thinks, *Uh oh! You're having a sensation. Something is wrong!* Rumination is an endless cycle of thinking about our thoughts, feeling things we think about, and thinking about the things we are feeling. So both our thoughts and our bodies are trying to get our attention simultaneously. Ignoring them or trying to change them may be counterproductive.

Sometimes, the thought combined with the feeling and the thoughts we have about those feelings start collecting other thought/feeling clusters similar to those that we have had in the past. In essence, a current thought/feeling triggers the historical sympathetic charges held in the body-mind that is in the same or similar energetic resonant field, amplifying the way that we're feeling and increasing the intensity and the number of those thoughts/feelings.

So if I were to see my reflection as I pass by a mirror and notice my belly hanging over my belt, my initial thought might be, *Oh my God, I am so fat.* And then that thought leads to the next, *I really need to get into shape,* followed by, *Well, what do you expect? Your diet is deplorable. I have no discipline at all. It's been months since I've worked out. How do I expect to find a relationship when I look like this? I am not sexy or desirable! Who in their right mind would want to be with such a lazy, fat slug?*

Each judgemental thought brings up a feeling of shame and self-loathing, compounding upon the next. Despair and disgust escalate into internalized disappointment and rage. At that point, I may begin to convince myself that there is no point in even trying to do anything about it because all of my attempts in the past prove that if I try to make a change this time, I'm only going to feel even more disappointed in myself when I don't succeed in losing weight. So why bother? I would just be setting myself up for failure. So, screw it, I'm going to eat a piece of cake. At least I'll have a few moments of pleasure. It's a vicious cycle of self-sabotage. And now, when I see my reflection, my eyes gravitate toward my muffin top, and the internal voice of shame victoriously reminds me that I'm a loser and therefore unloveable, so I might as well have yet another piece of cake. Hence, the self-fulfilling prophecy of confirmation bias.

Some new thought leaders (the irony of that moniker is not lost on me) are coaching their students that all they need to do when negative or unwanted thoughts show up, is to simply counter them with more desirable thoughts like, *I love my body. I am sexy the way that I am. There are plenty of people in the world that will find me attractive regardless of what my body looks like. I want someone who will love me for who I am, not for what I look like. Or, I have so much more value to offer someone than just what I look like.*

All of which are most certainly true. However, that method doesn't always work. Remember, you are in cognitive dissonance when you have a cognitive conviction that opposes an unconscious belief, regardless of whether the new thought is more positive in nature. Now you have two opposing thoughts. Opposing thoughts create a stress response and, consequently, palpable feelings of conflict and tension, which only adds to the previous ill feelings that the original negative thought brought to the surface. As soon as a thought or a life event hits the rearview mirror, it exists. It's now forever indelibly imprinted in your past; it's part of your story. So interposing a positive thought for a negative thought doesn't work because as soon as you complete the positive thought, it's now in the rearview mirror, too. It's also now part of your past—it's real, and it exists, too. Now you have these two thoughts that are real and exist and are in conflict with one another. That conflict now expresses itself as a feeling, too. And then, of course, you think about what the conflict feels like. And that is what I call 'The Spin Cycle.'

New thoughts alone cannot change beliefs, regardless of the number of times you repeat them. Think of how many times you have already had that old thought. You have reinforced and maintained that way of thinking for decades. So how many decades will it take to change that old neural pathway?

The thoughts that are part of your historical belief system, based on your early wounding experiences, will always hold more precedence because they have also been reinforced by the feelings and behaviors related to them.

And those same new thought leaders will tell you that the reason it is not working for you is that you have to also feel the emotion that you would have if that thought were to manifest the reality you want to have by thinking that way. So, stand in front of the mirror, look at your body, think that you are desirable, and imagine what it would feel like to be in someone's arms who loves you just the way that you are. Rinse, repeat ad infinitum.

Hopefully, in a few decades of consistent repetition, your new thought/feeling might be able to eliminate your old thought/feeling if you have also been able to win the war over the habituated shame spiral that you haven't changed or that it is taking you so long to do so.

Because the truth is, what is most real is what has already happened. Our past is undeniably our reality, even more than the present moment and certainly more than the future. The past is finite and real. It is immutable and unmalleable—its reality cannot be altered in any way, shape, or form. It exists. However, even though the reality of the past is ineradicable, your perception of it and your relationship to it can change.

The past is even more real than the present moment because the present moment is constantly fraught with perception.

In the present moment, your mind may be reliving a memory from the irrefutable past or projecting fantasy or, more likely, catastrophe into the hypothetical realm of the future. But once that moment has slipped even a millisecond into the past, it is seared into the dominion of the unchangeable. There is no option to choose to accept it or not, as it simply now remains as part of the tapestry of your personal story. And that is especially true for all wounding experiences, which are held in both implicit and explicit memory.

Personally, my reality exists solely in what has already happened and, to some degree, in what I currently see, hear, smell, taste, and feel. Beyond that, for me, it is all perception.

Everyone sees themselves and their lives through their own lens and filters that alter how they see, feel, and think about things. Perception is subjective and amorphous at best.

But, the fact is, the more fully oriented I am, simultaneously through all five of my senses, to the external environment, the more vastly heightened my connection is to that which is real in this moment. And the intensity to which I am, or am not, fully oriented to the space that I am currently in influences my engagement with my surroundings. But, if I have a cold and cannot smell the coffee, does that mean that, in reality, it has no scent? And how does my inability to smell the coffee affect my ability to taste it? Regardless of the coffee's reality, how much of my experience of it is based on my own capacity to engage with its various qualities?

Dr. Wayne Dyer once said, "Change the way you see things, and the things you see will change." If only it were entirely that simple. Granted, that shift in perspective is not without merit, but it may not be the whole picture. Most people think that if they change the details and circumstances of their outer world, they will feel different—like if I had six-pack abs, I would feel self-confidence. Again, that is true to some extent. Still, those internal changes may not be long-lasting, as the details and circumstances of our lives are constantly changing, regardless of the steely grasp of our efforts to control our external environment.

There is a more cogent reality. When we change the internal environment by healing wounds and returning to resiliency and self-reliance, then the external environment must reflect that. Then we can also show up in our lives in a different way. Change only occurs for most people when the pain of remaining the same is greater than the pain they anticipate that they will feel in making the change. Some people will stay in a toxic relationship because the fear of being single is greater than the fear of the pain they imagine they will feel in separating.

When a thought comes into your mind from out of nowhere, instead of imposing a different or more positive one or dismissing it outright, acknowledge it as a negative or undesirable thought. It's not just some errant, unwanted guest. It is here for a reason, so get curious about it. Maybe it has value and purpose. Perhaps part of its value and purpose is to create the sentient experience of the uncomfortable feelings to guide you into a deeper inquiry.

Instead of flooding yourself with positivity, try thinking, *I don't like this thought. I don't want it. It doesn't feel good. This isn't how I want to feel. This isn't healthy.* The negative feeling that arises as a result might even serve you as a source of inspiration to change a behavior, like heading to the market to buy healthy foods or taking five minutes to crank out a few sets of jumping jacks.

But most people don't want to feel their feelings, especially uncomfortable ones. They have the feeling, and want to get out of it, change it, distract themselves from it, disconnect from it, or simply dissociate. But let's see what would happen if, instead of chasing it away or running away from it, you lean into it. You let yourself feel it in as much detail and precision as you can. Give it all of your attention. Feel even the most subtle sensations in all of the different areas of your body that coalesce to create this experience. By becoming willing to feel the sensations that comprise the emotion, you will also find that the overall emotional expression becomes more tolerable.

If it begins to feel overwhelming in any way, you can shift your attention to a resource—anything that feels good in your body or something outside of you in the external environment that gives you a sense of well-being, calm, or safety. Let yourself remain there until you feel your system settle a bit. Then redirect your attention back to see how what you were previously feeling has changed.

In feeling the sensations with curiosity and willingness, ask yourself if there is anything old and familiar about how all of it feels. If this were to be a part of an implicit memory, what, if anything, does it remind you of? What did the thought bring up for you?

For example, if there is anything at all about it that feels old and familiar, then you might notice memories of the original wounds surface, or at the very least earlier reenactments of it. Stay with it. It's best not to rush the process. The longer you can remain focused and feeling, the more likely memories may come forward. You might recall a moment of being fat-shamed when you were quite young or being told that you were lazy.

However, images may not come up, as it is entirely possible that what you are feeling is an implicit memory—a precognitive memory of an event that occurred prior to explicit memory coming online. If you were burned badly when touching a hot stove as a toddler and scolded for doing so, it might lead to not liking to cook, which could explain your food choices, like prepackaged foods or eating at fast-food chain restaurants.

Take your time to just simply be with the sensations and the feelings of what happened. When you begin to feel a shift occur, perhaps a sense of relief or calm, then take time to feel into that. This is really important. The longer you can stay in the new feeling, the more likely the nervous system will reorganize and integrate what happened. Reorganization and integration are even more important than the activation (emotion) and discharge (your nervous system reprocessing the memory and releasing the stuck energy).

You might notice that your thoughts also begin to change during this stage. You may find new insights about the memory that you were reliving. Stay with these new thoughts. Stay with the feelings that they bring up. Revel and celebrate these new feelings and thoughts, which stimulate the release of dopamine.

From this new resourced place, you can imagine things the way that you would like them to be that could recreate the kinds of feelings that you are actually having now. And you can think and feel about that. What would that be like if you thought this other way or had these different and better feelings? In doing that, you will likely start to have even more of those feelings.

And now that you are in a new feeling state, it is time to take real action. What is one thing that you can do right now that would be more likely to create the experiences that you're daydreaming of? When you complete the action--celebrate the accomplishment.

This is when you really start to put neuroplasticity to work for you. Remember, when you are in the imaginal realm, you are in the perceived realm. And the lower brain doesn't know the difference between reality and your imagination if you are also simultaneously feeling it. And when you are in the imaginal realm, you are in the field of curiosity. Curiosity is playful. Playfulness and rewarding yourself create a dopamine-rich experience.

So each time you meet a negative thought, an uncomfortable feeling, or self-sabotaging behavior with curiosity, you have the opportunity to renegotiate and reorganize your nervous system response and heal old wounds.

A Narrative of Neuroplasticity

Let's take this analogy a bit further. Let's say losing weight is only one of the thought/feeling/behavior clusters that need to change so you can live a healthier lifestyle.

So as you stand in front of the bathroom mirror, sneering with contempt at your ample belly, you are overcome with feelings of disgust welling up inside of you. Your mind is riddled with the pervasive shaming thoughts about your lack of discipline, the generalized malaise of your ordinary life, and the long list of bad habits, like smoking, that you have never been able to break.

But now, you acknowledge that these thoughts and feelings are happening *for* you; it's not happening *to* you. You become willing to lean in and feel into the edges of the discomfort, not allowing yourself to plunge into the depths of the despair—but just enough—by feeling a few of the sensations that are a part of how you feel contempt, shame, or disgust.

Slowly and with precision, you notice your heart rate has increased, your chest feels a bit restricted, and your hands have gone clammy. Of the three sensations, you decide to focus on and get curious about the cool humidity on the palms of your hands. While doing so, you notice that tension around your chest is softening. Your body takes a deep breath all on its own, and you feel your shoulders drop. Until that moment, you weren't even aware that you were wearing them like earrings. You notice your feet are firmly planted on the ground and your legs feel toned and strong underneath you. Your heartbeat isn't even noticeable now.

You shift your gaze into the mirror and look into your own eyes and tears begin to form. You feel the warmth of self-compassion wash over you as the self-loathing fades away. You realize that you need to be more gentle with yourself. You also need to have realistic expectations. The changes that you need to make in your life will take time. You deserve more self-care in the interim.

Suddenly, you find yourself lost in a memory of floating on the still, azure waters of the Caribbean Sea, where you had gone to decompress after you made partner in the firm. Next, you are bombarded with just flashes of memories. You see your pre-COVID body dancing and sweating in a nightclub, having dinner that one time with the yoga teacher you had a crush on until you tried to have a conversation, trying on the 19th wedding dress that you knew was the right one the moment you turned to look at yourself in the trifold mirror.

And then you remember that you have always wanted to run a marathon. You begin to contemplate how you have thought for a long time that that would be such an accomplishment. And now you see yourself in your mind's eye crossing the finish line, exhilarated, and, at the same time, physically spent. You can almost feel the cold tickle of the tears of joy streaming down your cheeks, tasting the salt of them on the tip of your tongue while licking your lips.

With newly found grit and determination, you decide that you will commit to yourself once and for all, that you are finally going to do it. You chuckle to yourself, knowing that if you were to run a marathon today, you would end up in the emergency room. It's been so long since you have even gone on a hike. You don't even know when the last time was that you even saw your tennis shoes, let alone had put them on. Without a moment's hesitation, you find yourself spinning on your heels and marching your way to the jumble of your closet floor to dig them out.

But right now, you don't even have the time to walk around the block. You've got to get dinner started. On the way to the kitchen, you place your running shoes by the front door to remind yourself to put them on and go for a walk! You catch a glimpse of yourself in the entry hall mirror. This time, you pause and high-five your reflection.

As you begin pulling boxes and cans out of the overstuffed pantry to throw together a quick meal before the kids get home, you see all the Costco-sized prepackaged food in a different way. You hear the voice of the trainer that you had hired years ago to help you get into shape for your class reunion say,

"Food is fuel." At the time, it was everything you could do to resist rolling your eyes and blowing a raspberry. But he was right, and you have a marathon to train for! With a wiggle of your hips and an ever-so-slight shimmy, you happy dance over the fridge this time and grab Ben and Jerry by their Chunky Monkey and spike 'em into the garbage pail. Next up—a scavenger hunt to find the healthiest things you can to make something delicious and nutritious. A green bell pepper has never looked so good.

While the salmon is thawing on the cast-iron skillet you retrieved from the back of the bottom cabinet next to the dishwasher, you wave your hand over the veggies sautéing and relish the aromas of garlic, turmeric, black pepper, and paprika.

Once again, there's a wee wiggle of delight. "Mmm-mmm-mmm!"

As you open your phone and Google, *how to train for a marathon*, you mull it all over in your head, *I'm gonna run a fucking marathon.*

You're surprised at yourself for even thinking in such 'colorful' language—a memory bubbles up of your mom washing your mouth out with soap. You grimace, like Lucy tasting Vitameatavegamin, cock your head toward the ceiling, and jump up and down screaming, "Hey, Mom! I'm gonna run a fuckin'-fuckin'-fuckin' marathon!" Overcome with laughter and feeling like you can do whatever the fuck you want with your life, you bounce around and fist pump the air like a teenager at a rap concert.

Your husband and kids aren't sure what to do with you when they arrive home after baseball practice, smelling like—well, teenagers and a cigar. But you aren't quite ready to share why your hair looks like Sunday morning and, simultaneously, like the cat that swallowed the canary. This is *your* moment. The side-eye glances that you're getting are just enough to keep that smirk on your face as you play innocent as if nothing has changed. But something has changed. You can feel it deep within the seat of your soul.

Several weeks pass. Unbeknownst to you, your husband catches you doing a jig while vacuuming. He walks over to the wall and pulls the plug on your newly acquired YOU-SPENT-HOW MUCH-FOR-THAT?!?-Dyson vacuum cleaner. The blood rushes to your feet, and you feel immobilized, just like the time your father found your pack of cigarettes. The man, who you have never kept a secret from, takes you by the wrists and sits you down. With your chin on your chest, looking through your eyebrows, you rub your lips together while gathering your thoughts. Your hands twist in one another.

With expressionless trepidation, he asks, "Are you having an affair?"

"Um. Well . . ." You hesitate. "Why would you even think a thing like that?" But you're kind of liking seeing him like this.

"Oh, I don't know. You haven't hit the snooze alarm in I don't know how long. You quit smoking?!? You're running every day, and I'm losing weight. Don't get me wrong, I'm not complaining about any of that. But I haven't seen you act like this since we got married. I mean, *what's come over you?!*"

You sit in silence, and your eyes dart to the corner of the ceiling.

He collapses on the couch, sending the cat scurrying. He covers his face with his all-too-hairy hands and says, "I can't believe it. I can't believe it." He shakes his head in disbelief. "Actually, that's not true. I knew something was going on. *I knew it!* All the new clothes . . . a juicer, an air-fryer, a fancy-shmancy vacuum cleaner . . . yoga classes . . . and you're even meditating!" He gets up and begins pacing. "Seventeen years. For seventeen years, I've busted my hump for you and the kids. And how many times have you punched me in the shoulder because I noticed a beautiful woman walk by? How is this happening to me? How are you going to explain this to the boys?"

"Okay! Enough." You wave your hands like you are on the side of the road after having a flat tire, wishing you had actually paid attention when your father tried to teach you how to change one. You're barely able to contain your laughter. You roll your shoulders back, hold your chin high, and take a deep, resolute breath.

"Who is it? Your yoga teacher?! Oh Lord, please tell me it's not your yoga teacher."

"I'm going . . . to run . . . a fucking marathon!"

"You what? You're going to run a marathon? You're going to run a marathon." His eyes light up as they used to every time you simply entered the room. "You're going to run a marathon!"

You stand up. "I'm going to run a fucking marathon, baby!"

He takes you by the hands this time. "You're going to run a fucking marathon! Oh my God. Oh my God. Ah, Shnooks, that's amazing! Why haven't you told me until now?"

"Because I was afraid all of you would make fun of me. And, if I didn't follow through, I would just end up humiliating myself. But please don't tell the boys yet. I want them to see 'this old gray mule ain't what she used to be.' I want them to be proud of me. I want you all to be proud of me. Fuck, I want to be proud of me. And I can't wait to collapse into all of you after I cross the finish line."

"We'll all be there to catch you. I promise."

He takes you in his all-too-hairy arms, holding you tight, and lets out a long, vocalized sigh. You also sigh, but more like a balloon losing air. The two of you laugh together like you haven't done in entirely too long. The more you laugh, the more he laughs, the more you laugh.

He kisses away your tears of joy.

My Story of Joy

I had been so dissociative for so long, my sense of smell, direction, time, and the past had always been a bit wonky and unreliable. In the past, you could have walked up behind me and clashed cymbals together, and I wouldn't have so much as flinched. If I had seen someone in imminent danger, I would be immobilized and unable to move in any way or make a sound to get their attention, much less push them out of the way of a fast-moving bus.

At some point in the intermediate year of training to obtain certification as a Somatic Experiencing practitioner, I began to notice some bizarre changes. I had no idea what was happening to me. But it felt like something was wrong. Very wrong.

I began to exhibit a startle response. I didn't even know what a startle response was. But suddenly, if someone were to close their car door when I was walking down the street, I'd jump out of my skin and reflexively twist in that direction.

The shape of the sloping outer edges of my eyelids has always given me a bit of a sad appearance. However, I recall several years ago when I became aware of a slight glint in my eyes. Dare I say, maybe even a bit of a twinkle on occasion. The former blank, dead stare that I hid safely behind for so many years could no longer suppress the life force that began to resurface within me.

And I was no longer being constantly asked to repeat myself. People could actually hear me when I spoke. But to this day, a remnant remains. Oftentimes, when I introduce myself, people respond, "Nice to meet you, Brad." And if they don't hear Brad, they think I said Ryan. At 57, I still can't seem to pronounce my own name. Maybe it's the 'soft B' in Brian?

Of course, this isn't the only remnant of my former self that remains. I still have learning edges, growth edges, and healing edges to explore. Growth is an ongoing process, and the very essence of all life.

Not only had I begun talking with my hands like an overcaffeinated Latin, but now, my hands and arms seem to have a life of their own, like the inflatable dancing tube people that you see in car dealership parking lots. One night, while chatting with a group of friends at a bar, my left arm went flying helter-skelter, and I literally found myself having to apologize to a stranger for whacking him in the back of his head. I had transitioned from a six-foot-three zombie into a windmill missing a screw or two. Then there was that period of time when I was bumping into walls and knocking over furniture. I was a bull and the world was my china shop.

Could it be that I was becoming . . . animated?!

One day in class, I pulled my instructor aside. "Raja! Is it problematic that I don't have a problem? I mean, I just can't seem to dredge up any past traumas to work on in the dyads. I mean, it's like I'm so full—or over full. Like I just don't have a problem in the world."

"And you think that is problematic?" Raja quipped inquisitively.

"Well, I'm just on such a high. Like I've never been this high. Not even in the '80s in Manhattan, if you know what I mean," I said out of the side of my mouth.

"Don't worry, this is quite common," he tried to reassure me. "Your nervous system is coming back online. It may take some time to get used—"

I cut him off and rattled on, "No, you don't understand. I need to contain this. There's something wrong with me. It feels like

I'm having some kind of manic episode. Could I be becoming bipolar? Have you ever heard of that happening to someone from this kind of work?"

He slowed down his speech and spoke softly and deliberately as if he were trying to talk someone off the ledge. "This just might be your new normal. As your nervous system comes out of the chronic state of freeze, your banks of toleration will also increase. So, in time, your highs may be even higher, but your lows may feel even lower, too. This is what you want to have happen. You want to have a fully expressive nervous system. What if this were your new baseline? You don't want to spend the rest of your life flatlined, do you?"

"I don't want to end up on a park bench cackling like an idiot before they cart me away!"

He placed his hand on my shoulder and gestured toward the classroom. "Why don't you share this with the class. They need to see the positive polarity of this work, too. You seem . . . joyful to me."

Joyful?!?

That stopped me dead in my tracks. I hadn't even considered that it could be joy that I was experiencing. I wasn't sure, but it could be joy. I had never really felt joy before.

"So there's nothing wrong with me? There's something right with me? I don't know. I feel like I need to contain it. This just doesn't feel normal."

"Brian. Do you aspire toward normalcy?" He wisely left it there and walked back into class.

All the way home that afternoon, my mind was racing. *Could this be normal? Will I be able to learn how to harness all of this energy? Do I deserve to feel this much joy? Is this sustainable? How can I contain it?*

All I wanted to do was jump in the pool when I got home. Even the cold of the water felt different as I plunged in. It didn't send me to the surface, scrambling for the edge. Instead, I embraced it and hovered as close as I could to the bottom of the pool. My lungs braced under the pressure, but I relaxed into that as well, holding my breath longer than I think I ever had before. When I broke through the surface of the water, the sun was hot on my face. I felt alive—fully present.

For some reason, my eyes landed on a hummingbird resting and shimmering on a nearby geranium plant on the pool surround. I had never seen one sitting still before. I slowly lifted myself out of the pool and slithered, like Gollum, across the pool deck for a closer look.

As I got too close, it took off. But then it landed on the top of my head! My left pec started trembling in rhythm with its beating wings. I screamed for my partner, who came running out and attempted to swat the hummer off of me, thinking I was being attacked.

"No, no, no! Get the camera! Get the camera!"

This was long before the days of cell phone cameras, and by the time the camera could be found, once again, the hummingbird had taken off.

As I stood up, the hummingbird reappeared, hovering in front of my face. In shock and amazement, I gasped and took a step back as my hands rose up in front of me, palms skyward. It zoomed in a bit closer, and I wasn't sure if it was going to go after one of my eyeballs. But then *it landed in my hands!* Immediately, I thought to myself, There must be something wrong with this bird. I gently closed my hands, cupping it in a safe space.

Rodrigo returned with the camera, and incredulously, I exclaimed, "It's in my hands. I've got it. It's in my hands."

He fumbled with the camera like a four-year-old with a puzzle meant for an eight-year-old.

"Wait, wait, wait! Get that book. Get the book that Jennifer gave me for my birthday. It's on the coffee table."

A few weeks earlier, I had turned 40, and a friend had given me a book on animal totems. With the bird still in my hand, we literally cracked the book open to the very page on hummingbirds. The first line said that hummingbirds represent 'tireless joy.'

Tireless joy?!

It struck me that I had thought there was something wrong with it, and it needed to be contained, mirroring my exact words earlier with Raja about feeling joy. I felt time slow down. It was as if I were entering into some strange Jungian alternate universe. The symbolism and meaning couldn't be denied or explained away. And there wasn't any way that anyone would believe this. Unless I had photographic proof.

With the camera aimed, focused, and the shutter speed set, we were ready to capture what was most certainly going to be a blindingly fast departure.

"Ready? Set." I slowly opened my hands. "Go!" But it just sat there in my open hands, looking at the two of us as if we were the phenomenon. Clearly, there was something wrong with it after all. So I closed my hands around it again.

We called the Animal Wildlife Waystation and were given the name and phone number of the local hummingbird expert. She told me that hummers are federally protected and that I was obliged to bring it to her for triage care. She explained how to feed it with sugar water through a drinking straw and how to package it for the hour-long drive to Torrance.

I could barely steer the car; my hands were trembling so hard. I could barely see the road; my eyes were flooded with tears. What could this mean? It was all so surreal; I wondered if I was going to have another wreck. Did I have the angel of death in a Kleenex box sitting on the seat beside me?

But I somehow managed to make it all the way there. The hummingbird expert, a zaftig woman with a shock of red, tousled hair and the eyes of a child, deftly removed it from the box and nestled it deep in her ample bosom next to her heart.

After a brief moment, she shook her head and said, "There's nothing wrong with this bird."

My jaw hit the floor. "Let me tell you. *There is something wrong with that bird*," I said convincingly. "It landed on my head. It took off. It landed in my hands. *It stayed for a photo-op!* There's something wrong with that bird!"

"There's nothing wrong with her." She giggled.

I wasn't having it. I insisted that she keep the bird overnight for observation and promised to return in the morning if need be.

At 4 a.m., my phone rang. It was the hummingbird whisperer. She told me that the bird was fine, and I needed to come right away to pick her up because she might have babies to feed.

And so the story goes. I made the trek back to Torrance before sunrise to pick up Joy.

When I got back home and opened the box's lid to literally set Joy free, she just sat there. Looking deeply into my eyes, she cocked her head to one side with her wing crooked on her hip, as if to say, "Do you get it?"

I looked down at her with my mouth agape. Through teary eyes, I said out loud, "Yeah. I get it."

She shot up straight into the sky. She zigged one way and zagged the other, at which point she flew directly in front of the sun, and I was blinded by the light.

And she disappeared.

Resources

I hope you have enjoyed reading this book and that it has served you well. I trust it has helped you to build a strong foundation of knowledge and understanding about what trauma is, what the trauma of shame is, how you have formed beliefs as a result of traumatic experiences, and how those beliefs have created re-enactments, patterns, and vicious cycles in your life.

I have created an online resource file where are you will find some essential tools, skills, and other resources.

Tools, Skills, and Resources include, but are not limited to:

- Audio/Video Guided Meditations:
- The 5's Open-Eyed Moving Meditation™
- The Chair Meditation
- Effective higher brain hacks
- Physiology hacks
- Information on how to find support
- My YouTube Favorites List

You will have lifetime access. As time goes on, I will update and add more.

You will automatically be added to my book mailing list, which you can unsubscribe from at any time. However, if you choose to do so, you will not receive information about updates regarding the book, resources, or upcoming trainings.

Please visit:
www.BrianDMahanBook.com/Resources

Special Announcement:

I will be offering a follow-up live online training in the Spring of 2022, which will eventually be available for download as well.

Some highlights of what to expect:

- Explore the concepts of the book in greater detail
- Play with (not practice) the skills and tools
- Live demo sessions - volunteers will have sessions with me
- Q&A forums
- Create a tribe to support one another through the healing process

For more information and to pre-register,
please visit
www.BrianDMahanBook.com.
www.BrianDMahan.com

About The Author

Brian D. Mahan, SEP, is a wounded healer who found his way into this work initially as a client. And like you, perhaps, he is a complex person trying to live a simple life.

He is an author, teacher, lecturer, and a Somatic Experiencing Practitioner. He has been an assistant trainer of Dr. Peter Levine's Somatic Experiencing for two faculty members and is former assistant and teacher of the Lyon/Rubin Method for Healing Shame.

Currently, he has an international private practice, specializing in helping his clients heal from trauma and the trauma of shame. He holds in-person workshops and retreats and offers online trainings.

For more than 25 years, he has helped countless people from all walks of life. He has facilitated hundreds through an intensive detoxification and cleansing process, studied and practiced nine techniques of massage, and taught embodied meditation.

Following a catastrophic automobile accident in 2003, he began suffering from P.T.S.D. (Post Traumatic Stress Disorder). After working with a Somatic Experiencing Practitioner, his life and world shifted so dramatically and quickly, he was compelled to train in the same technique. Upon completing the three-year training program, his passion for healing and personal transformation shifted to working with people who suffer from developmental trauma, shame and shock traumas.

In tandem to his pursuits as a healer and educator, he has always written for personal and professional purposes. He wrote an award-winning (semi-finalist in Script Magazine's Screenwriting Contest) screenplay, *Heels and Humanity*, and wrote, directed and starred in the critically acclaimed theatrical production of *Time Lost*, as well as penning a few (un-produced) TV pilots.

He has garnered media attention in magazines and internet editorials, including being named one of *LA's Model Citizens by WNWN Magazine* and was profiled by *C Magazine* as an 'Urban Healer'. Other features include *DailyCandy, Yogi Times Magazine, LA Yoga Magazine, Healing Lifestyles and Spas E-zine, Sprig.com, TheRunDown.com, RealSelf.com, and LASPLASH.com*.

He has been interviewed many times, including *Better Together* with Maria Menounus, *Dear Gabby* with Gabrielle Bernstein, *Someone Gets Me* with Dianne A. Allen, HayHouseRadio.com with Lisa Williams, BlogTalk Radio's *The Bill and Kelly Show*, 2 interviews on KPFK's *The Aware Show* with Lisa Garr, and several podcasts.

For more information please visit
www.BrianDMahan.com
www.BrianDMahanBook.com